What Others Are Saying About

Listen to the Cry of the Child

"Barbara Hansen's *Listen to the Cry of the Child* is the story that had to be told. It will awaken in everyone a new sensitivity to this tragic problem of child sexual abuse so prevalent today. It will also bring hope to those caught in the web and open the way for deliverance and freedom. I urge every pastor and every church to take a proactive stance in promoting this book, and to deal honestly and courageously with the problem, no matter where it takes them."

—Anthony Bollback, Christian & Missionary Alliance—
District Superintendent (retired), missionary to China, author

"In *Listen to the Cry of the Child*, Barbara Hansen shows great courage as she opens her heart and shares her painful memories with her readers. Her healing and subsequent ministry through this book will be a great encouragement to others to break the silence that enslaves them. This book will prove to be a historical marker and instruction manual for the Church as it deals with sexual predators and the issue of sexual abuse. *Listen to the Cry of the Child* is a must-read for pastors, you[...] those who have experienced the violation of i[...] positive that God can and will restore what th[...]

—Rev. Timothy Horton, President and Founder [...]
Framingham, MA

More Endorsements for

Listen to the Cry of the Child

"In this vivid and heart-wrenching account of her life, Barbara Hansen exposes how the venomous tentacles of sexual abuse wreck havoc on its victims. But she also gives testimony to the beauty that Christ can bring out of such chaos. And now in her current ministry Barbara is a living example of the truth of 2 Corinthians 1:4, that God ' . . . comforts us in all our troubles, so that we can comfort those in any trouble with the comfort we ourselves have received from God.'"

—Scott Larson, President of Straight Ahead Ministries, author

"Barbara Hansen has a moving story to share—a story of God's remarkable deliverance and His marvelous healing. I feel certain this book will bring hope and help to many who have suffered in silence from sexual abuse."

—Charles W. Shepson, D.D., Founder of Fairhaven Ministries, author

Listen to the Cry of the Child

The Deafening Silence of Sexual Abuse

Barbara J. Hansen

WINEPRESS PUBLISHING

Packaged by WinePress Publishing, PO Box 428, Enumclaw, WA 98022. The views expressed or implied in this work do not necessarily reflect those of WinePress Publishing. The author is ultimately responsible for the design, content, and editorial accuracy of this work.

Front cover art and all pencil illustrations throughout this book by Jonathan Hansen.

Cover design by Josiah Williams, His Workmanship Design.

Author's photo on page 167 by PCA International, Inc. Used by permission.

Unless otherwise noted, all Scriptures are taken from the Holy Bible, New International Version, Copyright © 1973, 1978, 1984 by the International Bible Society. Used by permission of Zondervan Publishing House. The "NIV" and "New International Version" trademarks are registered in the United States Patent and Trademark Office by International Bible Society.

Scriptures marked KJV are taken from the King James Version of the Bible.

ISBN 1-57921-493-2
Library of Congress Catalog Card Number: 2002109803

DEDICATION

This book is dedicated to the love of my life, my husband Wayne, who never stopped loving me as God slowly brought me out of the darkness and restored me to wholeness.

I never could have written this book if you hadn't been willing to share our pain with others so they can find hope within their broken lives and marriages. And I never would have completed this manuscript without all your endless hours of help as I wrestled with the computer.

Thank you, honey. I have never stopped loving you ever since I fell in love with you under the blue Texas sky when I was seventeen.

Contents

FOREWORD

Journal Entry—New Year's Day, 1999

I am overwhelmed! Many times I have been questioned and criticized by the people I love the most—my family and my dear husband—because of the ministry I have to the "least of these." Only recently has my husband wholeheartedly joined my side and reached out with me to the deeply wounded because of the higher call of God on my life!

I feel so unworthy by the wonder of this call. In coming out of the darkness and going through all the rocky steps of learning, I have made mistakes. I have been cautioned by others, and more importantly, by God Himself. I am beginning to listen more deeply to His Spirit and go directly to Him instead of to others. I daily must confess all my insecurities and failure to Him in prayer. As I go to the Word of God and read the scripture, I gain His wisdom and knowledge to indeed "learn of Him." He is gradually and gently preparing me for this call. Do I question myself when I feel others are far worthier? Yes, but it is with dependability and in obedience to His Spirit that I am led.

I have been "checked" and "questioned"—many times to the point of tears—about my call. This call, by God Himself on my life, has been a very difficult one to obey. Then I remember how alone and deserted Jesus was when He carried our pain to the Garden of Gethsemane, and I know that He understands.

How could I be cheerful, joyful, encouraging others, giving a cup of cold water in His name (Mark 9:41) when my nights were pain-wracked and I was

9

awakened by God, who was my only portion to meet my insomnia and fear? I was scared and shaking (Psalm 55:5). I was worried and shaking, my pleasant evening became a night of fear (Isaiah 21:4). I would get out of bed and run to Him, like a little child trying to catch a butterfly in the warm summer breeze. I opened my Bible and read:

I am the Lord, your God, who takes hold of your right hand and says to you, Do not fear; I will help you.

—ISAIAH 41:13

There is no fear in [God's] love. But [God's] perfect love drives out [takes away] fear.

—1 JOHN 4:18

The Lord is with me; I will not be afraid.

—PSALM 118:6

He became my very portion, my support, my sanity, my peace, my hope and my security when I had no other support! For too long—from my perspective— His face seemed veiled, and my prayers seemingly went unanswered as I sought His timing, not mine. The next step or door gently opened and there was God, "I AM," to lead my steps as I trusted Him.

I am awed, humbled and even hesitant to say that God has empowered me with His knowledge and by His Spirit in this ministry. People who do not know Christ, have told me I am psychic. I would not dare to say such a thing. Psychic powers are not from God. His gifts are unique for His children. I am not fearful when I acknowledge that this gift has advanced my spiritual growth and my walk with my Father.

I am a very ordinary human being who has suffered abuse and betrayal, not unlike countless others. God Himself, this Man of Sorrows, who was all alone in the Garden when no one would even pray with Him, has daily prompted my spirit to continue to seek a filling that no human on the face of this earth can provide. It is only the miraculous power of the Holy Spirit that takes away suffering, loneliness, fear, panic attacks and anxiety in the life of this child! He has brought healing out of heartache and insists to my spirit that I should be a channel of love, joy, peace and hope in our broken sin-sick world. He continually assures me not to lose heart, despite my inadequacies, in my one desire to push others—those so desperately needy and lost in this world—to Him. In my passion to share this love as His servant, God can do immeasurably far more than I could ever do on my own as He continually fills my cup.

Now to him who is able to do immeasurably more than all we ask or imagine, according to is power that is at work within us, to him be glory.
—EPHESIANS 3:20–21

May this new day—this first day of the new year of 1999—be a beginning of new things in Christ for me, my family and friends as we seek to go deeper yet with God and to serve Him and one another until He comes back again!

The Lord is my light and my salvation—whom shall I fear?
—PSALM 27:1

I can do everything through him who gives me strength.
—PHILIPPIANS 4:13

Post Script

As you read this book, you will discover what a pivotal year 1999 became for me. I believe God honored the undercurrent of prayer in this journal entry.

God takes life's broken pieces
and gives us unbroken peace.

—Wilbert Gough

ACKNOWLEDGMENTS

With gratitude, I recognize some special friends who supported me in my journey to assimilate God's grace while I live in a broken "Humpty-Dumpty" world.

To my friends in the Berkshire Mountains of western Massachusetts:

Sarah Grosz—A once-in-a-lifetime friend, you saw beyond my wounded spirit and gave me the hope I longed to hear—the hope of expecting that God could bring good out of bad! Thank you, Sarah, for being faithful not only to listen to me, but also to cry with me and to wipe away my tears as well! I love you for giving me God's promising hope that I can expect His blessings and His peace. Thank you for your encouragement that God would use me in ways beyond my belief and that God would bring beauty out of ashes. You are my best, best friend!

Your encouragement helped me understand the truth of Joseph's observation in Genesis 50:20: "You intended to harm me, but God intended it for good to accomplish what is now being done, the saving of many lives."

Barbara Williams—As like-minded pastors' daughters, you and I encouraged one another throughout the several years of betrayal, denial, doubt, and recovery. You have allowed me to see myself as a "daughter of the King of kings!" We are now "dancing in the streets" with praise! I love you for being a special friend.

To the people at First Congregational Church of Hopkinton, Massachusetts:

Pastor Dick Germaine—Thank you for your challenging life-saving messages from God's Word since you became our pastor in 1986. And thank you for encouraging me to remain strong in Christ even when others fail me. As you shared from your pastor's heart your own vulnerability, growth, and maturity, you allowed me to give testimony to God's healing grace.

Paula (Menard) Minichiello—Thank you, my dear sister in Christ. You are the sister I never had. I appreciate your deep empathy and love, as well as your hope and prayers for me to "keep hanging on." I love you for your gentle prodding to be a "strong voice for victims" even when others were putting me down. Your encouragement to view myself as worthy of the "call" took me deeper into God.

Yvonne Magnussen—You have always been just a phone call away, ready to listen to a scripture God gave me or to share your wisdom and guidance. Thank you especially for your prayers. You validated my worth. I love you.

JoAnne Miedema—You were there for me when I was so broken I couldn't even tell you what was wrong. You understood the pain! Thank you for being my friend and for coming alongside me so many times when I doubted myself. I will always be thankful for the willingness of you and your wonderful husband, David, to quit your Bible study and begin one with my husband and me because we were hurting. Your faithfulness, your prayers, and the time you anointed my head with oil, giving me God's blessings, will never be forgotten!

Ruth Morrison—God sent you to me at a very critical time. You are a woman of prayer after God's heart! Thank you for telling me that I could call you any time day or night and just say, "Help." You promised to pray for me, knowing the Holy Spirit would tell you what to pray. Your encouragement, empathy, listening ear and mentoring me will never be lost. I will never forget when you gave me 1 Peter 2:20–21: "How is it to your credit if you receive a beating for doing wrong and endure it? But if you suffer for doing good and you endure it, this is commendable before God. To this you were called, because Christ suffered for you, leaving you an example that you should follow in his steps." That same day you told me you would be asking God for favor on my behalf, and from that day on He has given it to me. I deeply love you and Bill.

To my family:

My dear husband, Wayne—Honey, I never could have done this without your help! Thank you for bearing, hoping, and enduring with me during the intense, long sleepless days and nights as I wrote and edited my story! Thank you for allowing me to share our story of love that came out of the darkness of my emotionally painful and wounded spirit. I will always hold you very dear to my heart. I am so glad that we can laugh again.

I love you for standing by my side as God gently restored me to wholeness and as I moved into the fullness of His destiny and grace. Thank you for all the personal sacrifices and efforts you have given to this project, especially for the long hours on the computer when I didn't know what I was doing! Your endeavor to cheer me on may have fallen short if it weren't for your belief in me. You helped bring to accomplishment what God birthed deep inside my soul in spite of all the difficulties and pain.

When I think how far God has brought us in our thirty-seven years of marriage—as a couple, as a wife and husband, as a mother and father, as a team to mentor and support one another and others—it just amazes me! Thank you for pushing me to keep writing even when I didn't think I could write anymore. And thank you for releasing my spirit to fly!

Our sons, Todd, Brian and Jonathan—Through all the years we have been blessed to have you in our lives and to observe your growth physically, emotionally, and spiritually is praise I give to God for what He has accomplished in our lives as a family. I know it hasn't always been easy for you, but I have always known how much I am loved by each of you! And each of you is so unique to God and to your daddy and me. I love you dearly!

Todd, what a delight as a parent to hear you sing songs about God when you were only two years old and have you ask me, "Who put the clouds up there, Mommy? Jesus?" You were the first of our sons to invite Jesus into your heart at the tender age of three at vacation Bible school. Don't ever be ashamed to acknowledge your love for God.

Brian, when I thought my womb was barren, God blessed me with the gift of you. It was a challenge when you were little to keep up with your spirit. But what a delight to observe how God has multiplied your talents and is using the gifts that He has given you. I am moved to tears when I observe the similarities between you and me. Stay tuned to the Father and others as you empathize with "the least of these."

Jon, my gentle artist, musician, and poet son, thank you so very much for all your efforts and using your God-given ability to do the artwork to accompany my manuscript. Thank you, too, for patiently teaching me to use the computer and for allowing God to use you. I am in awe that you are willing to illustrate your mother's life!

> Sons are a heritage from the LORD, children a reward from him. Like arrows in the hands of a warrior are sons born in one's youth. Blessed is the man whose quiver is full of them.
>
> —PSALM 127:3–5

> Your sons will be like olive shoots around your table. Thus is the man blessed who fears the Lord.
>
> —PSALM 128:3–4

My wonderful mother and father, Rev. and Mrs. Charles Droppa— Growing up in a pastor's home was always such an honor for me as your daughter. Thank you for always having a place where I could feel safe.

Thank you, Dad, for leading me to faith in Jesus when I was only five years old. Although I have forgotten many of your sermons, I distinctly remember your prayers at my bedside and all your love, discipline, and teaching. I have vivid memories of walking from our parsonage next door into your study at the church. I probably should have knocked first because as I entered, I realized this was holy ground. You never corrected me for interrupting you, and you always made me feel like your little princess, as if I were the only one in the world who was important to you. Those memories are deeply imbedded in my mind. When I remember you on your knees looking up at me with those sweat drops on your strong gentle face as you wiped away tears, it is enough to bring this preacher's daughter to her knees even now. That wrinkled forehead, those tears, sweat drops, and prayers were just for me. You, my earthly father, must be a small touch of what I envision my Heavenly Father to be like.

Mom, I recall your faithfulness in giving me your "verse for today" that kept the Word in my heart when I wasn't digging for myself.

Thank you both for instilling in my being the practice of loving the Lord my God with all my heart, soul, and mind. Most of all, I want to thank you for loving one another, for your openness to learning about the devastation abuse caused in my life, and for building me up through scripture. You are the best parents a daughter could ever have. I deeply love you both more than you will ever know.

> From birth I was cast upon you; from my mother's womb you have been my God.
>
> —PSALM 22:10

> Train a child in the way he should go, and when he is old he will not turn from it.
>
> —PROVERBS 22:6

> Gray hair is a crown of splendor; it is attained by a righteous life.
>
> —PROVERBS 16:31

My brother, David—You were my hero, my knight in shining armor. I looked up to you and wanted to be just like you, so much that I copied everything you did. Thank you for taking my tiny hand in yours and allowing me to tag along with your friends. And thank you for sticking up for me and protecting me when I was still a wounded little girl. I am so grateful to God for answering my prayers and bringing you back to where God wanted you to be and to our family. I am blessed to have a loving brother as a part of my life. You are loved.

My sister-in-law, Sharon—I thank our Heavenly Father for bringing you into our family and for bringing us closer. You have helped me to believe that there is hope after the storm. Your e-mails have been such a blessing and encouragement. Thank you for loving me as a sister.

To all my extended family, including my daughters-in-law:

Thank you for caring about me and for giving me your gifts of books on recovery. I am thankful for all your love, and most of all for your prayers.

To my special friends:

Rev. Anthony Bollback, former interim, pastor of Friendship Bible Church, Keystone Heights, Florida, author and missionary to China— This book would not have been possible without your help as you allowed me to deal with those painful memories that happened decades ago. You were my lifeline to sanity during a time when I needed to be validated, listened to, and believed. As the chairman of the committee of discipline and restoration in my childhood denomination, you were my daily confidant via e-mails and phone calls. You wept with me and assured me that no stone would be left unturned. Because of the horror of the abuse, I had difficulty with authority figures, including pastors since one had betrayed me. You believed my story and were willing to help me face not only the person who abused me, but myself as well. Because you were willing to believe in me, I felt I could have the courage to believe in myself as well. Your true pastor's heart felt the deepest of empathy towards this pastor's daughter. I love you, Tony, and thank you for your help in editing my "Breaking the Silence" manuscript for the May 2002 issue of *Alliance Life*.

Pam Kokmeyer, my friend, the copy editor of and features writer for the *Falmouth Enterprise*—Thank you for your willingness to read my manuscripts and for the time you spent editing my testimony before it was published in a magazine. Thank you for never giving up on my abilities as a journalist and for being my faithful friend. We love you and René.

Athena Dean, acquisitions editor of WinePress Publishing—In August of 1999, when I first contacted you with my incomplete and very rough draft, you were open to my spirit and my writing abilities and told me to keep writing. I didn't even have the book written yet and was amazed and in wonder that you and your staff were willing to read what I sent you and to pray for me. You seemed to know in your spirit and sent me your prayer via e-mail: "In Jesus' name, will You open doors that no man could open, by the power of Your Holy Spirit to get the words that You want written onto paper!"

Thank you, Athena, for your encouraging e-mails and for sending me your book, *You Can Do It!*, and for calling and pursuing this author when I told you, "Now is the time." It was only two days later that I actually started writing this manuscript and five days later that it was completed. God bless you for your willing heart to be led by God's Spirit!

Sue Miholer, my new friend and editor of this manuscript—When Athena put us in touch with one another, who could have imagined the close bond of friendship and kindred spirit that developed almost immediately—you in Oregon and me in Massachusetts.

As we got acquainted via e-mail, we were amazed at the parallels in our lives. From 1950–1960 we lived less than a mile apart in Buffalo, New York. We found it unbelievable that your mother and her parents had attended my daddy's church before he went there as pastor. We discovered that we both knew some of the same parishioners. To think that we are only one year apart in age and that we attended some of the same area-wide church youth events and were in the same released-time class after school on Monday afternoons was simply fascinating. Could we have been friends?

Thank you, Sue, for the many hours you spent working so closely with me, for your prodding me to check on details and the sequence of events, as well as the potential reactions of those reading the finished product. Your integrity as I told you such intimate details of my life so you could get a better grasp of what happened to me and the fact that you didn't react with horror made me trust you more. Thank you for the friendship e-mails where we simply shared our lives with one another and our hurts and our concerns. I trust I will have the privilege of meeting you here on earth someday!

Judi Gage, a Lutheran pastor's daughter and my best childhood friend— An entire page should be written in honor of you. We told our "secrets" to each other all throughout our childhood. They surely would have been more terrifying had we not had each other to hold onto, like a cuddly, soft blanket. Sexual abuse was, and still is, a "dirty secret." And it was the admonition of "don't tell" that shoved me deep into denial and despair. But I told you, my best friend, and you had your "secrets," too.

We were ashamed by our secrets that we kept well-hidden except to each other. They were terrifying secrets, but thank God, I had you as my one, true friend who kept my secrets close to her heart, listened to me, and provided a safety net when I could tell no one else until well into my adulthood. You were always there for me. You laughed with me and cried with me.

We had the worst and best times of our childhood all mixed up in our minds as we dreamed and imagined things to entertain all the children in our neighborhood. We escaped into our imaginations by making haunted houses for the other kids, holding Uncle Sam parades complete with babies we pushed in their strollers, and putting on puppet shows and plays galore inside my father's garage, using my mother's curtains and selling the popcorn we made. We had fairs and circuses with prizes for the kids who always came expecting the greatest show on earth!

We played games like "Mother, May I?" and "Red Rover" into the evening hours. We started "The Pat Boone Fan Club," painted our attic floor red, buried our "treasures" in your father's old cigar box, rode our bikes to the zoo, and had our pictures taken by a real photographer to present to our dads on Father's Day.

The mental ward of the hospital was across the street from my house, and we sneaked under the fence to talk to the patients. We played in the forbidden woods on the hospital grounds and talked of dating and marriage. We never stopped talking because each of us had something to say and someone special who would listen.

One of the saddest times in my entire life was when your father took another church across town. We could no longer see one another a zillion times a day. The day my heart almost died was when my father took a pastorate way down in Texas. We moved there in my junior year of high school, and I didn't hear from you for many years. How could we lose touch when we had been closer than sisters.

Then one day, many years later, you sent a letter to my daddy's former church in an attempt to find me. That letter found its way to me. What joy to finally reconnect with you—the person closest to my heart who was ready to listen to any secret I had to share! Thank you, Judi, for still listening to my heart of hearts. We're still as close as any two best friends can be!

Rev. John Picard, Recovery Ministries, a part of Vision New England— Thank you that as you shared from a pastor's heart, you helped me realize that anger must be dealt with or it will destroy a person. Thank you, too, for being a phone call away when I needed it. You gave me hope to know God would someday use the gifts He gave me to honor Him. You have been such an instrument sent by God to partner with us in our ministry to those with life-controlling destructive habits.

Siegfried John Loh, a songwriter—You were inspired to write my song, *Victorious Survivor,* after you read my letter to the editor that told my story in the *Milford Daily News* in April of 2001. Thank you, Siggi, for so effectively writing it to let the world know that I am truly a victim no more because of God's love deep inside me and because of His healing power. Thank God He's touched my blind eyes and this child can now see.

To Jesus Christ, my Great Healer, and the One who made my manuscript possible:

You have brought "a crown of beauty instead of ashes, and a garment of praise instead of a spirit of despair" (Isaiah 61:3). "When anxiety was great within me, your consolation brought joy to my soul" (Psalm 94:19).

My complete restoration to wholeness in spite of the pain would have not been possible without my leaning on your everlasting arms. Thank You, God, for lifting my head, for listening to my heart cries, for restoring me to sanity, and for healing the darkness of my soul! You have "anointed me to preach good news to the poor . . . bind up the brokenhearted, to proclaim freedom for the captives and release from darkness for the prisoners" (Isaiah 61:1).

INTRODUCTION

TO WHOLENESS FROM WOUNDS
OF BROKENNESS

The Lord is close to [near] the brokenhearted and saves [rescues] those who are crushed in spirit.

—PSALM 34:18

I sought the Lord, and he answered me; he delivered me from all my fears.

—PSALM 34:4

Watching Oprah—October 1998

That day was a huge step of courage and freedom for me. After our son's wedding I was finally able to relax. Everyone except my parents had left our home. Dad was in a different room while my mother and I watched television. The *Oprah Winfrey Show* was on. I don't remember exactly what the program was about that day, except I do remember that part of it was about confronting your past. I admired the courage and boldness it must have taken on the part of those who were speaking. My mother and I were agreeing with Oprah and her guests about the importance of coming clean from whatever harm had been done to you.

I remember thinking to myself, *I wish I could do that! How I wish I could openly tell my mother about being molested by an older family member.* But the secret of that hideous humiliation had been locked inside me by tremendous shame. Years of doubts and fear had bound me for decades!

How come I don't have that kind of courage? What is it going to take for me to tell? Questions I had asked myself over and over again.

Keeping the Secret

My mother was now in her early 80s, and I was an adult, thirty-three years into my marriage. Just that summer I had mustered all the courage I had and finally told both of my parents about the youth pastor who had sexually touched me when I was eleven and twelve at a church youth camp all those years ago.

But, this deeper secret plaguing me was too close to home because it involved a family member. The secret had been buried for a long time, but it was now creeping to the surface. What energy it took to keep it under wraps! Would my mother believe me anyway if I told her? Besides, I was living with the fear my father had impressed on me when I told him about the family member just three years earlier. He had said, "Don't tell!" Funny, that's exactly what that relative told me after he molested me so many times. It felt as if I were being victimized all over again by my own father. He went on to say, "You can't tell her; it might kill her!"

"Daddy," I said at the time, "I know without a doubt that she was also a victim!" Two of my relatives had already told me they had also been victims of this same person. I knew from what I had read that child molesters don't stop at one victim. They usually hurt many in their family.

The sad part was that this dirty little secret lying just beneath the surface was killing me!

Suppressed Anger Surfaces

An abuse victim suffers in silence. By remaining silent, and with the fear of anyone discovering my "secret," the effects of the abuse on my adult life were sometimes far more devastating than the actual abuse! I had been trying for years to get free from my addiction to a life of denial!

When *The Oprah Winfrey Show* was over, I turned off the TV and my mother went upstairs. Soon my father came into the family room and began to chide me about my ministry to those "crushed in spirit"—the drug addicts, alcoholics, prostitutes, ex-cons—those people the world sees as throwaways. I think he was concerned I might be putting myself in jeopardy and it was his way of saying he cared about my well-being.

God had just begun to give me His heart for those who were in that kind of darkness. My husband and I had gone into a minimum-security prison and a crack house to minister. We had started to mentor those steeped in their addictive lifestyles. For the very first time in my life I was beginning not only to feel tremendously deep empathy for all of God's children He created, I was also able to bring the wounded to the Great Physician who is able to meet all of our needs and free us. Isn't that what the Bible teaches? And isn't that what I had heard my dad preach from the pulpit for years?

Seven years before this incident, I attended a ten-session course for abuse survivors that had been helpful as far as information, but it didn't really get to the issues I needed to address in my life. When the topic of anger came up in one of those classes, I couldn't identify. I didn't see myself as an angry person. But what I failed to see was that unless anger—whether it shows outwardly or is deeply suppressed—is dealt with, it has the ability to destroy you! When it is released, it doesn't mean that those horrific memories are forgotten; it means that you are released from the hate that has settled inside your soul.

Suddenly on that day in that room with my father, all of the suppressed venom, like poison from a viper, came out with an overflow of tears and sobs that I didn't even realize were coming from me. I had never acted this way and was so afraid my mother would hear me. I heard myself say, "Daddy, you don't understand! The pain the people I work with are in is the same as my pain; they aren't any different than me! Why can't I tell my mother? This relative is dead. I did nothing wrong to deserve my being so dead inside my soul!"

Pandora's Box Is Opened

By now I was weeping as my mother came back downstairs, thinking my father and I were arguing. I heard my father say, "Maybe you should tell her now." Words I never thought I would hear. They would free my spirit forever.

I immediately ran to the basement where my husband was working. I grabbed his arm and told him, "Pandora's box has been opened! You'd better come upstairs, because I'm about to tell mother the dark, dirty secret of my past."

The Sins of the Fathers

> He does not leave the guilty unpunished; he punishes the children and their children for the sin of the fathers to the third and fourth generation.
> —EXODUS 34:7

I sat weeping, grieving deeply for the loss of my childhood innocence. I also realized the importance of what was about to happen in relation to the healing of my family. I took my husband's hands as well as those of my father and mother. They were intently looking at me, wondering what I was about to reveal to them. I started by telling my mother that I was a victim of abuse, not only by a youth pastor, but also by someone very close to her who was a family member. Before she could respond, I went on to tell her I believed that she, too, had been a victim of this same person.

My dad, not wanting to hear the facts, put his hand on her arm and questioned her, "Honey, it didn't happen, did it?" She nodded that it had indeed happened. As my father looked at her with disbelief, she said to me, "Why, oh why, didn't you tell me years ago?"

What Fear Does

Fear chokes the soul just as weeds choke the most beautiful flowers in the garden. Now, as this fear was beginning to be released, perhaps the garden of my life could start blooming just as it had been created to do by my Creator.

> There is no fear in love. But perfect love drives [casts] out fear, because fear has to do with punishment [involves torment]. The one who fears is not made perfect in love.
> —1 JOHN 4:18

> But I will rescue you on that day, declares the Lord; you will not be handed over to those you fear.
> —JEREMIAH 39:17

> But now, this is what the Lord says—he who created you, O Jacob, he who formed you, O Israel: "Fear not, for I have redeemed you; I have summoned [called] you by [your] name; you are mine. When you pass through the waters, I will be with you; and when you pass through the rivers, they

will not sweep over you. When you walk through the fire, you will not be burned; the flames will not set you ablaze [scorch you]."

—Isaiah 43:1–2

Post Script

Although the word picture is not original with me, I see fear as the wrapping paper around the gifts from God that are inside you. You must go through the fear, embrace it, and then discard it to discover what is inside. When fear comes uninvited, it needs to become an offering to God and to yourself to work through that fear in order to free your soul to live.

Do you flee . . . or can you cast aside the wrapping and unwrap the gift?

A Life Shattered by Abuse

Woe to that person through whom they come. It would be better for him to be thrown into the sea with a millstone tied around his neck than for him to cause one of these little ones to sin.

—Luke 17:1–2

Family Life

My family was one of those "Kodak moment" families. We learned to respect God and one another. God entered almost every conversation and, to the best of their ability, my parents set a good example.

Growing up as the daughter of a pastor, I was given deep spiritual roots by my loving parents. At the age of five, realizing that Jesus loved me, I prayed to receive Him into my heart.

Prayer at bedtime and other times during the day, vacation Bible school, Christian camp, youth group, church and a daily family altar were a normal part of our lives. If our friends came to our home during our family altar time, we always included them. It seemed that we were always in church whenever the doors were open. I loved God and the things I was taught. I

loved going to junior church where I learned Bible verses and songs and heard lots of Bible stories taught by my favorite teacher, Mrs. Mowry, who had a spirit of joy.

My best friend Judi lived on my street. Life was good!

My home was very loving, but it was also a disciplined and authoritarian home. I didn't get spanked much, but I remember that my brother was taken to the coal cellar at times. Listening through the heater grate to him being punished is still a very painful memory for both my mother and me. He is two years older than I, and I adored him. He was my protector and my friend, and I copied everything he did because I wanted to be just like him—a mirror image. But he was the leader; I was the follower. He was the straight-A student; I struggled with school.

The Abuse Begins

I can't remember when the sexual abuse began, but it was when I was a very little child, maybe as young as two or three. The "secret" of this close family member molesting me while treating me to ice cream was unthink-

able! *Favors are always given to the victim. It is a way to hold power over him or her, downplaying the abuser's part in the abuse and hoping the innocent child won't tell.* I did not. He told me not to. I was too little to understand anyway.

I felt very unprotected and very vulnerable at this older family member's home. This relative entered my bath time without the knowledge of anyone else in the family. He exposed himself to me numerous times. He also took me alone with him in his car where he molested me.

Recently I was listening to a call-in program from Boston where listeners were encouraged to call in about the molestation of victims by Catholic priests. One woman called in and said something like: "At least children are safe on Santa's lap." As soon she said that, I had a flashback. This relative used to dress up as Santa to pass out the presents at our family's Christmas gatherings. I knew he wasn't the real Santa. I knew the real Santa wouldn't molest me in front of other family members while I sat on his lap wearing my pretty holiday dress.

When I was around eight, I decided I'd had enough and would teach him a lesson! When our family went to his house, I didn't hug or kiss him hello or goodbye. I hoped no one would ask me to. They did not. That ended the abuse . . . until three years later at a Christian camp.

My life was forever changed by the abuse of two people who should have loved and protected me, and not harmed me!

The Second Abuser

"Shhh! Don't tell!" This is what the stocky and balding twenty-seven-year-old youth pastor told me as he gave in to his uncontrollable urge to molest me. He singled me out, as if picking the sweetest, ripest, freshest, undefiled orange at the supermarket. The details of those events are as vivid in my memory as if they happened yesterday. He fondled me underneath my black tank bathing suit while he laughed and joked at the swimming hole! When everyone around us thought we were having fun, he whispered in my ear: "This is our little secret; keep it to yourself; don't tell!"

This sent up a warning sign: *Don't let him get too close!* And it also raised a question: *Why is he doing this to me?* This time I knew it wasn't OK. I struggled and nearly drowned. Hanging onto the dock, I kicked to free myself from his advances. I have had a fear of water ever since—and I don't like ice cream either!

Secrets are a pedophile's biggest tool. Children need to be taught there are OK secrets (keeping a surprise birthday party a secret) and "go and tell" secrets (when someone who touches you inappropriately tells you not to tell anyone).

My parents trusted everyone, thinking I was safe from predators, not realizing that these child molesters—who they knew—were hurting me and others, luring us all into their deceitful web.

I had heard my mother say many times how safe this camp was. She thought it was like "hallowed ground" (a term I actually heard her use) where she and other pastors' wives didn't have to worry about allowing their children to wander "free and innocent" because "everyone was watching everyone else's children."

Oh, indeed, you were watching us, weren't you, Mr. Evangelist? All those summers you put on your mask as a musician, songwriter, song leader, altar-calling youth pastor, you were really watching us, weren't you?

Back in the 1950s, parents didn't instruct their children about "good" and "bad" touch. Nor did they talk about sexual abuse with their children—and probably not with each other either. My parents had warned me about not accepting rides with strangers, but the family member and the youth pastor were not strangers. Dr. Dan B. Allender, author of *The Wounded Heart*, notes the "eighty-nine percent of abuse occurs by someone known to the victim." *The sad fact about incest is that victims always trust, love and know their abusers.*

The Results

As a young teenager, I felt lifeless inside but didn't know what was wrong with me. I was filled with shame, so scared and sad that my smile became forced. I had few close friends, and my schoolwork suffered. I struggled with math and history; I just couldn't connect with those subjects. I studied so hard for tests, but because of the abuse and the chunks of memory it forced me to blank out, I had an extremely difficult time remembering information for tests. I resorted to cheating just to pass. But I liked English, literature and writing and did well in those subjects. (I never dreamed I would become an author, but it shows that God can make something out of what appeared to be nothing) Then, as I grew into young adulthood, I felt as if a wrecking ball had come down on my head and shattered my life like a mirror into a million pieces all over the road of life. I have been trying to pick up the pieces of my life ever since. *Oh, here's another piece over here and another over there,* I would say to myself. Piece by piece, I picked them up, thinking it was all my fault! Just like all the king's men in "Humpty Dumpty," I had no idea how to put myself together again. This huge puzzle with its scattered pieces—my life—had been created in the image of God, but in my shattered state, it was impossible to realize that image. I had been betrayed, and because of that betrayal and the thirst the perpetrators had to "feel good," I will never be the same!

Held Hostage

Sexual abuse held me hostage for over forty years. *You don't have to be in prison to be a prisoner!* Huge chunks of my memory were blocked out, coupled with an inability to cope. The mind protects itself until one day all the ugliness spews out like the hot river of lava flowing down the mountainside, not caring who or what is in the way! You become like a Vietnam War veteran or a Holocaust survivor who blocks out those painful memories. You've had horrific things done to you, or you've been made to do or see things at a young age you never should have done or seen.

I couldn't talk about it for decades. When the flashbacks came, I spent a tremendous amount of energy shoving them back down! It was a nightmare and nobody, including my family, knew that something was terribly wrong. It felt like a living hell. I felt like I was living a lie. I was filled with guilt and wanted to forget but I couldn't.

I was mortified at the age of sixteen when I hadn't started my monthly cycle. My mother had to take me to the doctor for hormone shots to make my body begin doing something that should normally have started by that time in my life. No one questioned what was wrong. Who would have suspected it was because of the sexual abuse. I certainly didn't!

When my husband proposed to me, I told him about the abuse. I was afraid not to. *But people who have not been abused cannot begin to understand how little they understand.* I didn't talk about it to anyone else.

We tried for four long years to get pregnant and were unsuccessful. My doctor sent us to an infertility clinic where they did all kinds of tests on both of us. Nothing seemed to be wrong with either of us. No one asked if I had been sexually abused. Why would they? But I knew something was terribly wrong.

The pain of keeping this dirty little secret buried took an enormous amount of energy, and it took a tremendous toll on my body. My body's reaction was not unique.

Victims of sexual abuse—male and female—become stuck in both an emotional and physical timeframe. The body shuts down physically and emotionally, and actually becomes unable to function as it should.

> Let me not be put to shame, O LORD, for I have cried out to you; but let the wicked be put to shame and lie silent in the grave.
>
> —PSALM 31:17

> He heals the brokenhearted and binds up their wounds.
>
> —PSALM 147:3

My Journey Out of the Ashes

God said He would "comfort all who mourn, and provide for those who grieve in Zion—to bestow on them a crown of beauty instead of ashes, the oil of gladness instead of mourning, and a garment of praise instead of a spirit of despair" (Isaiah 61:3).

Early Pictures

As a little girl I was intensely shy, quiet, very trusting, withdrawn and extremely vulnerable. Every time I see a picture of me around the age or five or six I feel quite sad. I am never smiling. I see a lot of hidden pain in my face and a voice that couldn't speak about what had happened to me. Like a deaf mute, I became silent about it for decades, desperately wanting to tell someone what was happening in my silent world of memories, but unable to do so. Like the silent falling of the snowflakes, no words about it came out; no voice was heard. I was like a choir that couldn't sing. There was only the silence of my "deaf" world. I had ears and a mouth, but I could not speak the unthinkable. I screamed but no sound came out of my mouth. There were only tears late at night when no one but God was listening.

Although I wouldn't remember it in the morning—and not even now—my mother tells me that when I was about five years old, I would sometimes wake up in the middle of the night screaming hysterically. She knew I had had a nightmare and as she picked me up, she'd assure me that "Mommy is here. You're OK." I looked very frightened and would kick her while I sobbed hysterically and screamed, "You're not my mommy!" She recalls that I looked so very, very scared that it frightened her terribly! She would hold me close and pat me for about half an hour until I went back to sleep.

As I grew into preadolescence, I looked undernourished and almost anorexic. The signs are all there in my pictures—pictures I don't like seeing. I drank milkshakes to gain weight and didn't understand why I was so skinny. I never gained weight and I never liked the way I looked. I didn't go through puberty when my friends did. (I needed hormone shots to make that happen) I thought I was ugly.

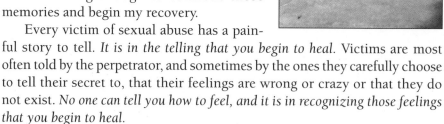

While my girlfriend Judi blossomed into a lovely teenager, I had to stuff my bras with toilet paper! I knew something was terribly wrong but didn't know what it was. (I discovered later that the abuse shoved me—and my body—backward instead of forward) I never felt normal or adequate until much, much later. That happened only when I took a long and painful journey to my past and became strong enough to confront those memories and begin my recovery.

Every victim of sexual abuse has a painful story to tell. *It is in the telling that you begin to heal.* Victims are most often told by the perpetrator, and sometimes by the ones they carefully choose to tell their secret to, that their feelings are wrong or crazy or that they do not exist. *No one can tell you how to feel, and it is in recognizing those feelings that you begin to heal.*

Coming Out

The hardest part of my coming out of the closet of abuse was telling my family. By 1995, my father, my husband and my children knew, but it became "our secret." I desperately wanted my mother to know. When the older relative who had abused me died I didn't even shed a tear. He was never a relative to me anyway. But he was a respected member of his community and an elder in his church. *An abuser often leads a double life, portraying himself to everyone as a fine upstanding citizen. The truth is known only to the abuser and his victims.*

When the relative who had abused me passed away, I wrote this poem:

Letting Go

Today they buried the abuser
And with it all my fear—
Of sadness, tears and all the abuse
Year after year after year.
Today they buried the abuser.
Healing has already begun;
I am a victim no longer
Through Jesus Christ, God's Son.

Because my dad had told me to stay silent about being abused by this relative, I remained numb and in denial for another three years. Even though this relative's death provided me some relief, the fact was that the secret was killing me and keeping my imprisoned soul bound!

The "shedding" or "coming out" came in bits and pieces. An elderly saint who counseled me during this time gave me this advice: "Don't open that door. When God wants it open, He will open it." That took the pressure off me.

When the son of the relative who had abused me died, which was after that day in 1998 when I told my mother of the abuse, it all came to the surface during a family gathering after the funeral. I decided to speak up because by then I knew that both the older man and his son had molested other family members as well. I was criticized for telling, and some people in my family said they never wanted to see me again! I was dumped on and victimized twice and was told, "Put the past in the past; put it at the cross"— as if praying about it would get rid of the pain. Why wasn't it OK to come clean? I had done nothing to cause this sin. Didn't Jesus set an example for us when He set the captives free? Satan knew what I was about to do in exposing evil since he is the prince of darkness. I had to choose at that moment whether to listen to the people in my extended family or to obey the voice of God. In this world of sin we are to expect persecution if we are to follow the call of God. My only desire was to bring the needy and weary to faith in Christ through it all. The call was a heavy one—like the sound of a distant drum.

The Sovereign Lord has given me an instructed tongue, to know the word that sustains the weary. He wakens me morning by morning, wakens my ear to listen like one being taught. The Sovereign Lord has opened my ears, and I have not been rebellious; I have not drawn back. I offered my back to those who beat me, my cheeks to those who pulled out my beard; I did not hide my face from mocking and spitting. Because the Sovereign LORD helps me, I will not be disgraced.

—ISAIAH 50:4–7

When you are abused, you are repeatedly told not to tell. That sent me deep into a decades-long world of mute, deaf and numb silence. Anyone who has never been abused cannot fully understand why we aren't able to tell until many years later. I have been asked why I didn't tell. *I just couldn't— not until the time that God opened that door.*

The Journey Out

During my journey out of the darkness I literally devoured scripture and books on recovery. Some books were too raw and painful to read, especially those whose authors had suffered severe abuse at the hands of those who were supposed to love and protect them. The details of my abuse are not necessary except to say that one inappropriate sexual touch can be as devastating—and send the victim into a downward spiral of doom—as if that person had been raped. Mine was more than a touch. When my best friend from childhood recently asked me if the abusers had raped me, I answered simply: "They raped my soul!"

My belief system was betrayed and shattered in order to protect the family. I had been taught to always tell the truth, but this time I wasn't allowed to. "Shh . . . don't tell," the abusers reminded me often. Somehow protecting the family by not telling the truth trumped all other values during those long years of my silence. My boundaries were violated by the very adults who were supposed to protect me.

Part of the belief system I grew up with was that once you accept Jesus, the past is gone and should be forgotten. That is not true. Only when it is remembered, embraced, confronted with truth rather than lies can we find the courage to come completely out of denial. But we need to know what the truth is, and it is found only in our God who saves our wounded spirits.

As I use the lens of God's truth found in His Word to look at the false beliefs I grew up with, I am beginning to see myself in His perspective rather than in my own. Fear versus faith. Lies versus the truth. Fear is hard to let go of, and we need the truth in order to be whole. When we let go of our fear and own insecurities we can cling to God's still, small voice speaking to our spirits, saying, "You are not alone . . . I will lead you . . . you can trust Me . . . I am able to heal you."

The Root of Sexual Abuse

Sex offenders who target children have often been sexually violated themselves. Some grew up with very domineering or controlling parents. Others were raised in abusive homes or had at least one alcoholic parent. And some grew up in families that manifested more than one of these dysfunctions.

Whatever their upbringing or life circumstances, they are filled with deep insecurities and rage. Some kill; others commit suicide. I had no desire to do either. In fact, I now have deep empathy toward those who abuse because it is a reflection or manifestation of their painful pasts. They cross boundaries and use their power and control over innocent little victims to meet their own perverted needs. From the beginning of scripture, God warned about the generational curse that is passed on from one generation to another:

> Yet he does not leave the guilty unpunished; he punishes the children and their children for the sin of the fathers to the third and fourth generation.
> —Exodus 34:7

Sexual abuse is an addiction to unnatural sex, something that was practiced by the perpetrator who abused me. This very often brings about codependency in the abuser. He becomes dependent on someone or something to fill that deep hole or void brought about by his own abuse. *Only God can fill that void.* Abuse is always a sickness, and it is always sin. *Jesus is the only One who can take it away.*

Hope for the Abused

Hope comes only as the layers upon layers that have been built up over the years are uncovered. The memories must be brought to the surface to be validated and understood. Those memories act as a life preserver for the victim, much like what we would offer a drowning swimmer who is struggling to make it to shore.

The only way *any* of us—the abuser as well as the abused—find the approval we seek and discover our worth is to spend time with God our Father. To allow someone other than God to be the source of that approval or determine our worth is to put that person in the position of God. *Abusers operate from that position of power.* God gave me so much hope and His promises as I began devouring the Word of God and began the slow healing process. Again and again, I was drawn to Psalm 10:14–18: "The victim commits himself to you; you are the helper of the fatherless. Break the arm of the wicked and evil man; call him to account for his wickedness that would not be found out. . . . You hear, O LORD, the desire of the afflicted; you encourage them and you listen to their cry, defending the fatherless and the oppressed, in order that man who is of the earth, may terrify no more."

Denial vs. Embracing

Denial of our past is to deny God. To face our past and embrace the truth is to live.

First Corinthians 13:11 says, "When I was a child, I talked like a child, I thought like a child, I reasoned like a child. When I became a man, I put childish ways behind me."

If you or your loved ones do not understand that scared little girl standing in the corner holding her blanket and sucking her thumb, you will never understand the lonely, fearful adult who is angry and confused and silenced by years of denial. That is what happens as long as the victim continues to be victimized by denying the abuse.

The abuse victim needs deliverance from that kind of bondage. Deliverance means that the thing that used to control a person has now been put under God's control. We are controlled either by this world and the things in it or by Jesus Christ. Although we cannot change our pasts, they do not have to be in charge of us!

I refused to be intimidated or silenced any longer about the bondage of abuse. God has raised me out of the ashes and I am becoming a strong woman of faith. I am experiencing victory over wrong, realizing that good overcomes evil and that Jesus will reign over the devil.

My Ministry

Some people want to put me in a box, and some are threatened by me, but they don't understand. (I was never in a box to begin with!) Because of my past, I have an intense calling to intense people who have been brutally wounded by this world. It is a path I never would have chosen for myself, but God has moved me from being a back-seat wanderer to become a front-line Christian. There is a side to me that some do not understand. They don't understand how I want to minister to those who are so broken. But I've surrounded myself with a couple of very close friends who support my goals and encourage me to grow. I am so fortunate that God has brought my life-partner and my best friend—my husband—alongside to join me in those goals. They have become his goals as well since God has healed our marriage!

The Lord began quietly speaking to me when I was alone in my quiet time with Him. In reading the story of Samuel's obedience to God I was struck by the similarities to my own situation. God calls us. "The Lord called Samuel" (1 Samuel 3:4). *Are we listening?* "Speak, for your servant is listening" (1 Samuel 3:9) was Samuel's eventual answer. Sometimes God has to repeat His call as He did with Samuel. It took three times before Samuel answered.

When God began to solidify His call on my life in early 1999, I told my husband I knew there had to be a purpose for my existence and that I had to find out what it was.

His response was: "Barb, you are a wonderful wife and mother."

"No," I said, "there is a greater purpose for my life and I have to find out what it is!" God's voice was like the sound of a distant drum. It was a sound I tried to deny, but I had no choice but to listen to it.

Sometimes in our uncertainty or stubbornness, or in our insecurity or unresponsiveness, we ignore the call. *Are we afraid to act? Do we think God will fail us?* "He [Samuel] was afraid to tell Eli [the priest] the vision [God gave him]" (1 Samuel 3:15).

Are we hiding something? Eli reminded Samuel that God knows when we are hiding something. "Do not hide it from me. May God deal with you, be it ever so severely, if you hide from me anything he told you" (1 Samuel 3:17).

We need to be honest with one another—and especially with God—since that is the only way to freedom and peace. When we are obedient to His call, we can depend on His leading to yield fruit in others and in us.

> But he knows the way that I take; when he has tested me, I will come forth as gold.
>
> —Job 23:10

My surrendered need becomes His unlimited opportunity. My Father is the God of recovery. He restores our souls to health.

God found you, as if you were cast away as a baby, unwashed, unclean, uncared for and exposed to ridicule. No one had pity or compassion on you and you were destined to die by this world's standards. But God calls you to *live*. He sees you as you are, not as you were, and as what you can become!

—EZEKIEL 16:4–8 (MY PARAPHRASE)

LOVE THROUGH ADOPTION

THE GIFT OF A MOTHER'S LOVE

Sons are a heritage from the LORD, children a reward from him. Like arrows in the hands of a warrior are sons born in one's youth. Blessed is the man whose quiver is full of them.

—PSALM 127:3–5

I prayed for this child, and the LORD has granted me what I asked of him. So now I give him to the LORD. For his whole life he will be given over to the LORD.

—1 SAMUEL 1:27–28

The Desire for a Child

Like Hannah in the Bible, my womb was barren. I related to Hannah. Those were negative times for both of us. My barrenness brought back memories of the abuse. Hannah's situation was intensified by the irritating heckling of her husband's second wife.

Hannah's husband asked, "Why are you weeping? Why don't you eat? Why are you downhearted? Don't I mean more to you than ten sons?" (1 Samuel 1:8).

After four years of marriage, we, too, desperately wanted a child. We had so much love to give. And similar to what Hannah endured, we had to suffer some cruel and insensitive remarks. I was heckled by an older woman in our church who was ignorant and had no right to ask me, "Why aren't you pregnant?" But she did! Hannah cried and prayed. So did I!

There seemed to be no reason why I wasn't able to conceive. My husband and I were both healthy and had jobs that were very fulfilling. My gynecologist sent us to an infertility doctor. We tried for four years to conceive, trying many, many different and difficult ways to achieve conception. We were told nothing was wrong.

Many of our friends were becoming pregnant. We yearned for a child. It was hard for me even to go into a department store and see mothers pushing their children in strollers or walking hand-in-hand with their toddlers. I couldn't even go in the baby department without walking out crying. No one understood the pain I was in except my husband. I just wanted to become a mother! Every month we came up empty. If children are a gift from God, why were we not having one? God knew Hannah and I were grief-stricken and answered both of our prayers in His time.

> So in the course of time Hannah conceived and gave birth to a son. She named him Samuel, saying, "Because I asked the LORD for him."
> —1 SAMUEL 1:20

Adoption?

One day in my doctor's office, I started asking questions about adoption: "What do you have to do? Is it hard to get a baby? How much does it cost? Where do we go?"

My doctor answered my questions as best as he could and then added, "Don't try so hard; relax. You don't want to have two children on your hands!" My mind interpreted what he said to mean that perhaps we were thinking about it way too much, and he didn't want us to adopt, relax, and *then* get pregnant.

We called adoption agencies. They sent us information. Their lists of requirements were long. They'd have to do thorough home studies, and ask about our marriage relationship, our families' relationships, and how we'd raise or discipline our child. And there would be a zillion meetings with social workers. My head spun just thinking about it!

It takes a very special mother to bring another mother's baby into her home. Not every person is cut out to be an adoptive parent. The challenges that come are very different from those of the biological mother. Older children who are available for adoption come with a very good chance that they have been abused or neglected. If you adopt an infant, there is the unknown of genetic disorders or the problems that a baby can have because of the mother's lifestyle choices while she was pregnant.

We thought about it, talked about it and concluded: "You never know what your natural-born child will be born like anyway, do you? And you don't send *them* back!"

When you adopt, you invest everything you have in you to give. But the rewards are great! The greatest gift of love someone can give is to adopt a child. The most unselfish act though is the gift of love the birth mother gives—the gift from inside her heart and soul!

Our Son Is Born

The phone rang. I answered it. It was my gynecologist's nurse calling. She asked if my husband was home? She and the doctor wanted to talk to both of us. I told her that my husband was away on a business trip and asked if there was a problem.

Finally she broke the news to me: "We have a mother who is a patient of ours who wants to give up her baby for adoption. We called you first because you recently expressed a desire to adopt a child. The mother is due to give birth in three months. She is Catholic, but her only requirement is that her baby be placed in a home that desperately wants and will love her child! You must seriously think about it and talk with your husband. If you aren't positive, there are others on my list that I can call."

As I hung up the phone, my hands were shaking. My heart was pounding. I began to cry. This was a direct answer from Heaven from a God who heard me and was answering my prayers! He gave me an angel who was willing to give us her own flesh and blood, and the gift to love her child.

I could hardly wait to tell my husband. What would he say? What would we do? Could we really take in someone else's child?

There would be no red tape, no home study, no long applications to fill out or questions from nosey social workers to answer. Without a doubt, this baby was literally dropped in our laps by God. We couldn't believe the miracle of answered prayer.

Hannah's prayer and song to the Lord in 1 Samuel 2:1–2 became mine as well: "My heart rejoices in the Lord; in the Lord my horn is lifted high. My mouth boasts over my enemies, for I delight in your deliverance. There is no one holy like the LORD. There is no one besides you, there is no Rock like our God."

A birth mother has nine months to prepare for her child. We had three. It was such a happy time of joyful anticipation for us. We couldn't believe it. We busied ourselves getting the nursery ready, painting it yellow because we did not know the sex of our anticipated child. My neighbors had a surprise baby shower for me and my church threw an even bigger one.

I knew no other adoptive mothers, so I had no one with whom to compare notes. I had so many thoughts going through my head. But we knew we had made the right decision. We were choosing to love this baby, which is the most sacrificial gift two parents can give their child.

In the lazy, hazy heat of the summer of 1969, our first son was born to two very inexperienced and excited parents. We named him Todd, which means *watchful*: "But watch thou in all things, endure afflictions, do the work of an evangelist, make full proof of thy ministry" (2 Timothy 4:5 KJV).

I wept when he was handed to me for the first time at the hospital, as I became his mother when he was only five days old. His little tuft of hair was blonde, just like his father's, and we fell in love with one another instantly. He was an easy baby.

Post Script

Within five months, I was pregnant with our second son. We named him Brian, which means *one of strength*: "The Lord stood with me, and strengthened me. . . . And the Lord shall deliver me from every evil work, and will preserve me" (2 Timothy 4:17–18 KJV).

I prayed for one and God gave me two. According to 1 Samuel 2:21, Hannah also went on to have more children—five more!

LEGACY OF
AN ADOPTED CHILD

Once there were two women. . . . . Who never knew each other.

One you do not remember. . . . . The other you call Mother.

Two different lives. . . . . Shaped to make you one.

One became your guiding star. . . . . The other became your sun.

The first one gave you life. . . . . And the second taught you to live it.

The first gave you a need for love. . . . . The second was there to give it.

One gave you a nationality. . . . . The other gave you a name.

One gave you a talent. . . . . The other gave you aim.

One gave you emotions. . . . . The other calmed your fears.

One saw your first sweet smile. . . . . The other dried your tears.

One sought for you a home that . . . . The other prayed for a child, she could not provide and her hope was not denied.

And now you ask me. . . . . Through your tears the age -old question

Unanswered through the years. . . . . Heredity or Environment?

Which are you a product of?. . . . . Neither, my darling, neither.

Just two different kinds of love!

(AUTHOR UNKNOWN)

45

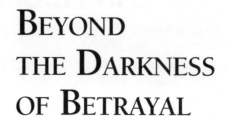

BEYOND THE DARKNESS OF BETRAYAL

Whoever survives a test must tell their story; it is their obligation to helping others.

—HOLOCAUST SURVIVOR

When you make a vow to God, do not delay in fulfilling it. He has no pleasure in fools; fulfill your vow. It is better not to vow than to make a vow and not fulfill it.

—ECCLESIASTES 5:4–5

Broken Vows

When I had looked deep into my young husband's eyes and said my vows on our wedding day in 1965, I meant them: "for better or worse, in sickness and in health." I quoted Ruth 1:16 in my wedding vows when I told him: "Where you go I will go, and where you stay I will stay. Your people will be my people and your God my God."

I never dreamed in a million years that I would personally be faced with an affair on the part of my husband after only nine years of marriage. Satan tried to rob us of what I honestly thought was a marriage made in Heaven. The pain sent me reeling! I felt like the rug had been jerked out from under my feet!

I have my husband's permission to tell our story because it is a story of God's forgiveness and grace. The only reason I write about it now is to give other couples hope that they too can not only survive but also come to fullness in a love for one another once again.

When it happened I was utterly bewildered. My trust in people, particularly in men because of the sexual abuse, was already shattered. But I was so in love with my husband and trusted him unbelievably. He was my protector, my provider, and the love of my life!

My husband and I had been through much testing and many ups and downs in our marriage, beginning with our inability to conceive that involved years of infertility. On the other end of the spectrum was the complete joy of adopting our first-born infant son and then giving birth to our second son.

The Affairs

The eye of the adulterer watches for dusk; he thinks, "No eye will see me," and he keeps his face concealed.

—Job 24:15

I believe that not only sin, but also circumstances led to the affair. When our older boys were almost two and almost three years old, my husband's father committed suicide. I never realized how deeply devastating that horrible experience was for my husband. In a way, I believe he felt his father's suicide was his father's ultimate act of abandonment. He didn't talk about it with me at all, and I saw him cry only at the funeral. I believe that his intense pain, much like my abuse, turned inward into denial. He became like a turtle inside this big, thick shell. *When pain is not dealt with, it festers like poison or a sliver under the skin. If pain is not dealt with, it will come out either verbally with anger or inwardly with denial, which is anger on the inside of one's soul.*

The details of the affair are unnecessary. No one knew what we were experiencing, least of all us.

With persuasive words she led him astray; she seduced him with her smooth talk. All at once he followed her like an ox going to the slaughter, like a deer stepping into a noose till an arrow pierces his liver, like a bird darting into a snare, little knowing it will cost him his life. Now then, my sons, listen to me; pay attention to what I say. Do not let your heart turn to her ways or stray into her paths. many are the victims she has brought down;

her slain are a mighty throng. Her house is a highway to the grave, leading down to the chambers of death.

—PROVERBS 7:21–27

Any form of infidelity requires us to be dishonest with ourselves, with others, and with God. And dishonesty poisons our lives, making our walk with God impossible. His warnings are severe. Lust leads to the death of our spirit's ability to relate to God's Spirit. If we do not seek repentance and forgiveness, it can also lead to spiritual separation from God.

My son, keep your father's commands and do not forsake your mother's teaching. Bind them upon your heart forever; fasten them around your neck. When you walk, they will guide you; when you sleep, they will watch over you; when you awake, they will speak to you. For these commands are a lamp, this teaching is a light, and the corrections of discipline are the way to life, keeping you from the immoral woman, from the smooth tongue of the wayward wife. Do not lust in your heart after her beauty or let her captivate you with her eyes, for the prostitute reduces you to a loaf of bread, and the adulteress preys upon your very life. Can a man scoop fire into his lap without his clothes being burned? Can a man walk on hot coals without his feet being scorched? So is he who sleeps with another man's wife; no one who touches her will go unpunished.

—PROVERBS 6:20–29

I felt like I had no one to talk to. No one I knew had suffered the devastation of an affair. I felt like my husband had taken my heart and stomped on it. I also had great difficulty understanding how he could have given that part of himself to another woman. My foundation of what marriage meant to me was ripped out from under me. I felt dead inside!

Why be captivated, my son, by an adulteress? Why embrace the bosom of another man's wife? . . . The cords of his sin hold him fast. He . . . [is] led astray by his own great folly.

—PROVERBS 5:20–23

If I thought I couldn't survive the first affair, within a year it happened again. This time I knew I couldn't handle this burden alone. I carefully chose a person I thought would keep my confidence. I was wrong. I told my secret to a married friend who must have told someone else.

One night I got a phone call from an acquaintance in the very small church we attended that nearly destroyed me! "Barb, I thought you two had a good marriage." She went on and on, asking, "How could your husband have done this to you?" Instead of tenderly holding my severely broken heart in her hands, she was throwing arrows at it.

The woman who had the affair with my husband also had a prominent position in the church. We knew the young pastor and his wife well. I found out several years later that the pastor knew of the affair, but because he was naïve about how to work with couples in crisis, instead of coming alongside us, he did nothing.

Nothing + Nothing = Nothing

Anything would have been better than nothing. Years later, when I had the courage to talk to him, this pastor apologized to me. He requested my forgiveness for his insensitivity and inability to deal with someone who was going through the intense pain of betrayal. I gave him my forgiveness.

But, when the affair happened, I felt shunned and rejected by my own church family. I felt we had no choice but to leave the church. Besides, how could I face the woman who had betrayed me? I was so frightened but told no one. I had so many questions I could ask no one: *How in the world could I heal? What had happened? What if a pregnancy resulted from this affair? Was this going to keep repeating itself?* I felt like my world was upside down and my marriage had failed and was at my feet in shreds.

> Like a bird that strays from its nest is a man who strays from his home.
> —PROVERBS 27:8

A New Start

We began attending another church. I called the pastor and invited him over. We told him about the problems we faced and were open to any answers he might have. He had none. Instead, he told us of the struggles he had with lust but gave no solutions to salvaging our broken lives. He simply listened to us and prayed with us.

The thing that temporarily saved me was that my husband's company promoted him and we got to move away from everything. I made the mistake of simply forgiving my husband, telling myself that "love protects." I don't know where I heard that phrase, but in not dealing with the severe pain of betrayal, I had simply put a bandage on a festering wound.

Forgiveness doesn't just happen. I now realize that premature and quickly granted forgiveness can actually hinder the healing process. Although I forgave him, I didn't know how I could ever trust him again.

When our hearts are ripped out of our chest, our spouse needs to hear and feel the pain. If he or she doesn't know how deeply you are hurt, the pain will come up in everything and anything you say or do. *It never goes away on its own.* If your spouse does not understand the depth of the pain that he or she caused, you will be stuck in grief and never be able to trust or love your spouse again. As with my denial of the sexual abuse, my grief once again turned inward. My spirit was crushed and I felt like it had literally died. *Trust has to be earned in order for forgiveness to come from the heart.* That, too, would take time for me. But it didn't fully come for another twenty-six years of marriage, not until I came face to face with myself. I call it "looking in the mirror darkly." And I didn't like what I saw in the mirror!

Another Issue

Another thing that played a part in our marriage problems was pornography. It wasn't hard-core porn, but the results are the same. It is like inviting a third party into your bedroom, even if it is only looking at another woman's naked body in a magazine. *Pornography in any form has no place in a marriage.* Porn is another form of cheating, whether it is viewing it on the Internet, going to a strip club or a peep show, looking at *Playboy* or having an affair.

Because God sees and knows our hearts, we are never alone, even when we think we are. If you are having a problem with porn, you need to ask yourself two questions: *Would I look at this with my wife by my side? Am I turning outside my marriage to get something that I can get inside my marriage?* We all need to be honest before our God, our spouse, and ourselves. Look inward to see what need in your life porn is filling. *Porn is an addiction.*

My husband and I began reading books on this subject. As we read *An Affair of the Mind* by Laurie Hall and *The Silent War* by Henry J. Rogers, we began to reconnect with each other. After his second affair, my husband sent me an e-mail with the following verse, making it his promise to me: "I made a covenant with my eyes not to look lustfully at a girl" (Job 31:1). It was a promise that let me try to trust him, and it gave me hope.

Another Child

Soon after our move, I became pregnant with our third child. We named him Jonathan, which means *God's gracious gift*: "The LORD make his face shine upon thee, and be gracious unto thee" (Numbers 6:25 KJV). He was an easy baby and a delight. He gave both my husband and me great joy and made my days very busy. About six weeks after his birth, I entered into a spiral of darkness that enveloped both my soul and my spirit. It went much deeper than "the baby blues."

I had little time to myself and I felt all used up. I was afraid to reveal my real feelings of inadequacy to anyone. I cried a lot and slept only a little. When I consulted my doctor, he didn't know how to treat me except to tell me that maybe I needed to talk with a psychiatrist. I didn't want anyone to tell me I was crazy.

My doctor prescribed Valium, which made my depression, sadness and severe anxiety even worse. I never felt like I would harm my children. Even now, I have a hard time really understanding how a mother could kill her own flesh and blood. Although the bond between a mother and her precious babies does not correspond with harming them, I do understand the highs and lows after birth that come with hormonal changes. But very few people back then understood what we now know about postpartum depression.

Postpartum Depression

According to W. David Hager, M.D., and Linda C. Hager, M.A., in their booklet on postpartum depression, written for Focus on the Family, researchers have found that between fifty and sixty percent of mothers experience a mild form of postpartum depression, called by many "the baby blues." Although many mothers experience mood changes caused by the sudden changes in hormones in the mother's body after pregnancy, only twelve to fifteen percent of those experiencing the baby blues are found to have significant depression that qualifies for the diagnosis of postpartum depression. Unfortunately, up to fifty percent of these cases go undiagnosed because the mother never seeks medical attention.

Deborah Sichel, M.D., an expert in postpartum depression and psychosis, mentioned on *The Oprah Winfrey Show* during November, 2001 that one out of three women suffers from some kind of postpartum depression. She and Jeanne Watsen Driscoll have shown how depression and anxiety result from long-term chemical "loading" as the brain repeatedly "revs up" in response to stress—in this case, the stress of a pregnancy and the responsibilities of caring for a newborn.

According to the National Institutes of Health, postpartum depression happens in ten percent of all pregnancies and typically develops within the first few weeks after childbirth.

The definition of the term probably is the reason for these differing statistics, but it appears that postpartum depression in one degree or another affects between ten and thirty percent of all new mothers.

I was one of them, but because none of my friends knew what I was experiencing, I felt all alone.

My Mother's Gift

My precious mother gave me such a special gift during this horrible time for me. It didn't even cost her a thing; she simply did it out of love, and her gift was priceless to me. Knowing that I wanted to run away from all my responsibilities, and sensing that something was drastically wrong with her daughter, she simply said, "Come. I'll take care of you and your children." It was like life to my weary bones in a body that had run dry. I drove the three hours to her house. Like a little lost girl, I wept when I saw her and ran to her loving arms. She took care of everything while I slept late, ate whenever I wanted to, nursed my infant son, and played with our six-and seven-year-old sons. While I read and took naps, my delighted boys played by their grandmother's feet. She knew exactly what I needed. Mothers are like that. I temporarily got well, but the pain that was so well-hidden from even myself still had not left my heart.

> A man's [woman's] spirit sustains him [her] in sickness, but a crushed spirit who can bear?
>
> —PROVERBS 18:14

It wasn't until almost thirty years later that I realized this depression had everything to do with what had happened in my life. Those suppressed memories of sexual abuse in my childhood, the sexual abuse during my preadolescent years, as well as the betrayal in my marriage were all a part of my postpartum depression.

Not until 2002 did I tell any of my doctors that I had been molested. And that was only because I had finally come to grips with what happened to me and slowly came out of the darkness. This is one of my primary reasons for writing this book: I want others to come out of the darkness. Yes, my fears were many, but I have clung to God's promises. I am drawn to His Word like a duck to water.

Never will I leave you; never will I forsake you.

—HEBREWS 13:5

So do not fear, for I am with you; do not be dismayed, for I am your God. I will strengthen you and help you; I will uphold you with my righteous right hand.

—ISAIAH 41:10

In the prime of my life must I go through the gates of death and be robbed of the rest of my years?

—ISAIAH 38:10

The LORD will save me, and we will sing with stringed instruments all the days of our lives in the temple of the LORD.

—ISAIAH 38:20

Pivotal Spiritual Life Conference

We made another move around this time. It was a God-ordained move that started the process of restoring mental, emotional and spiritual wholeness to our marriage. A change of companies and a new direction for our lives gave us both hope and discouragement. But for the first time in my life, I began to come to grips with the deep issues of betrayal and abuse.

The pastor of our church suggested we attend an upcoming spiritual life conference—Congress 1985. We thought it might be one put on by the church's denomination, but found that it was sponsored by Vision New England, a regional spiritual renewal ministry. About 8,000 people from all walks of life and all denominations and backgrounds were there. Speakers came from all over the world and there were several seminars from which to choose.

David Seamands, author of *Healing Damaged Emotions,* was the keynote speaker and spoke on "Incest, the Family Secret." His message was meant just for me. He gave several statistics about sexual abuse and then used Luke 13 as his text. In that chapter, Jesus touched a woman who had been crippled by a spirit of sickness for eighteen years and was bent over. When

Jesus touched her, she was set free from her infirmity and immediately straightened up and praised God. He further explained that he felt this woman did not have an evil spirit and postulated that something had happened to her in the past that had given her this spirit of infirmity. He said we could do nothing about our past and went on to explain that memories we suppress will cripple us and can be used by Satan to destroy us. The alternative is to give them to Jesus and be healed.

We can decide to become bitter, or to become better. In the Bible, when Joseph's brothers sold him into slavery, he endured abandonment by his family for about thirteen years, according to Bible scholars, as well as false imprisonment. But in the end he was able to say to his brothers, "You intended to harm me, but God intended it for good" (Genesis 50:20).

Dr. Seamands explained that our minds are like computers with the ability to retain everything—both the good and the bad. The choice is ours to do what we want about those memories and how we live. Our minds and emotions are affected by what we have experienced, thus influencing our total personalities.

When we choose not to deal with some of those memories, we are limited in reaching our full potential; our relationships with people are limited; we are easily hurt, suffering from low self-esteem; and we become crippled Christians. Satan uses unresolved guilt to keep us from reaching our highest potential.

David Seamands came from a family of missionaries to India. During Hitler's regime, he became separated from his parents when he was only eleven years of age and didn't see them again until he was twenty. He had angry, pent-up emotions because of those nine years of separation. He said that he, like I, had held onto the anger of those circumstances for a long, long time. It was only when he faced those memories and dealt with them that he became freed from them.

Listening to his message was like life to my veins. The message was riveting and spoke just to me. I had never heard any kind of message about sexual abuse or about the importance of not ignoring our memories in my life.

I began crying like a baby. *I was that woman and needed Jesus to loosen the bondage that had me bound for decades! I needed a touch from Him!*

I came home from that conference stunned, not knowing what to do or how to heal. I was enveloped in grief—grief from my past that had never been dealt with, grief from all that I had experienced, and grief that I was not where I should be spiritually, emotionally, physically and mentally. I went to God in prayer and began reading my Bible in a way that I had never done before. I began to experience a holiness from Him that was unlike anything I had ever felt. He began to speak to my broken, wounded spirit.

My Spiritual Non-Growth

I read Revelation 3:8: "I know your deeds. See, I have placed before you an open door that no one can shut. I know that you have little strength, yet you have kept my word and have not denied my name." Then I read further in verses 15 and 16: "I know your deeds, that you are neither cold nor hot. I wish you were either one or the other! So, because you are lukewarm—neither hot nor cold—I am about to spit you out of my mouth."

Whoa! That was me! My spiritual life was cold! Yes, I believed in Jesus. I had accepted Him into my heart as a five-year-old when I prayed at my daddy's knee, but my spiritual life was practically non-existent. My mother wrote letters to me, faithfully sending me verses on a weekly basis. I'd read them sometimes, but I was not digging on my own.

No wonder my emotional life was topsy-turvy! Our minds, bodies, wills and spirits are all connected and need to be nourished. I had prayed for years for my husband to be the spiritual head of our family, but that was a poor excuse for my own wayward living.

Spiritual Hunger

The Holy Spirit began a new work in me at that time that has literally changed my dark spirit. The embers from the fire were there, but not the burning with the fire from God that I so desperately wanted and needed.

Within less than two weeks of my spiritual renewal, God spoke to my husband. I began to observe a spiritual hunger in him, too. The change I had prayed for in my husband's life had to begin with me. I have learned that it never works when we set out to change our spouse, our kids or anything around us. The Holy Spirit has to change me first.

The deeper I got with God, the more hunger my husband had for Him. God was beginning to answer my prayers!

The Lord will keep you from all harm—he will watch over your life.
—PSALM 121:7

SEVERE TESTING

I n 1990, my husband began to experience severe testing in the area of his health. Our boys were in their teens and early twenties. We were approaching our mid-life and looking forward to more time together. I was beginning to devour books about sexual abuse and infidelity. I even got up the courage to share some of these with my husband.

He was overloaded with stress at work and began to use the word "hate" in reference to his job. He had little authority at work, but did a lot of paperwork in order to keep others happy. He had a hard time saying "no" because he felt a need to please and do for others, but in the process he neglected himself. (I realize now that I did much the same thing)

By 1992, his health issues started to overwhelm him. He became very anxious and fatigued. As a field engineer, he was a troubleshooter, someone who knew how to fix problems. But he felt like he, too, needed "fixing."

Search for Answers

His doctor had made an initial diagnosis of diverticulitis by 1991. But something more was wrong, and my husband began making appointment after appointment with many doctors—eventually fourteen over a three-year period. He had various tests at the hospital, but the results always came back negative. He was troubled by his health problems and it showed in every area of his life. Even our friends noticed a change in his behavior.

The fullness he felt in his stomach kept him up at night. He'd wake up in the middle of the night and spend several hours sitting or kneeling. Sleep would not come. One morning he told me he had a clawing sensation in his stomach as if something were trying to come out.

He once told me, "If I start doing or saying anything funny, get me help immediately! I don't want to do something crazy like my father did!" That scared me. I was sure he was suffering from a nervous breakdown. He couldn't do anything except drag himself to work every morning. I was doing all the physical work at home, and the mental and emotional pain got to me too. He thought he had cancer or that maybe he had AIDS. He and I both got tested for HIV. What a nightmare! Thank God, those tests all came back negative!

A woman's self-worth is related to her home and her children. But because a man's self-worth is greatly tied to his work, this preoccupation with his very real health issues affected his ability to be creative and feel good about himself.

He analyzed every area of his life and could not accept it like it was. He was tested for every imaginable physical problem, but nothing clicked. He was unhappy and had no purpose or joy. One evening he spoke to me harshly, saying, "I can't meet your emotional needs when I can't even meet my own!"

I thought the worst: *Is he having another affair?* He was not. I called his boss to beg time off for my sick husband. He went to our pastor who prayed with him and gave him a book about mid-life crisis.

Our marriage was at a standstill and he began the "name-blame game," saying I was the cause of his physical problems. I was humiliated because I felt all used up with nothing left to give. That drove me deep into anger. The problem was not mine, but he was making it sound like it was.

I'm sure he felt all used up too because we were both desperately searching for answers, and no source we consulted had an answer for either of us. Neither of us had a clue what the other needed, which was intimacy and a caring heart for the other. There were days when I was very sad and felt so empty. We spent almost no quality time together and simply existed in the same house that seemed so empty for both of us.

No one, nothing, or no substance of any kind can fill that hole that only God can fill. His Spirit must connect to ours.

How I Felt

I began writing him letters and tucking them in his briefcase so he could read them when he had time. In those letters I expressed my emotions and communicated my feelings without blaming him or justifying my actions. I wanted him to hear me with both his head and his heart, to get inside my shoes and understand how I felt. It had become too hard to talk about these things without the discussion getting heated, and that accomplished nothing. The letters allowed me to give up control and begin to love and take care of myself so that I would eventually be able to love my husband more deeply. In this way, I began to take responsibility for my own behavior and in time it released my husband to begin to take control of his life instead of feeling all used up with nothing left to give.

In August of 1993, I wrote in my journal:

I am anxious and confused over our marriage. We are having conflicts and avoiding one another. I want to talk and be open. He's closed and withdrawn. I don't feel he is being honest with me anymore. What if I was the one who was sick? Would I get his support? I am optimistic; he is pessimistic. I look at the cup as half-full; he looks at it as half-empty. I have support from my friends, but I desperately miss my husband! He wants my support and sympathy for his illness. I don't feel like I have anything left to give! I feel zapped of energy to give him. I have stopped asking how he feels because I can read it on his face. He is so negative. I miss his jokes, his laughter, his playfulness with me. Some days I don't even like my husband! What an awful thought even though I'm in love with him.

Another entry the next month reads:

A good friend said it's like living with a spouse who has a chronic disease—or like living with an alcoholic. She suggested I go to Al-Anon meetings. Mid-life should be more fulfilling and I should have fewer responsibilities now. He's not happy! I'm not happy! Doesn't my husband realize he could lose me? I wouldn't fight to keep him anymore like I once did. I guess I don't feel I have the energy, and wonder to myself: Is it worth it anyway? I wouldn't want to be totally alone, although I feel all alone anyway! He is grouchy and sharp with me. I react! He worries and says every area of his life is affected. He doesn't "deliver" anymore. I call it "empty promises." He is driven into himself and seems unfocused to everything. Oh God, what do I do to help him?

A journal entry from January of 1994 pretty well sums up how I felt:

I am tired of the whole illness that has been first and foremost in our mar-riage in the past four years. I see him jumping to everyone's aid, constantly being a helper (which he says is his creative nature), and I don't see how he can help everyone when he is the one who needs help! His doctor told him two years ago that he worries too much. His response at the time was: "I am just anxious and fatigued." When will it ever end? Is it exhaustion, chronic fatigue, severe depression, thyroid problems, a nervous breakdown, mid-life crisis, sleep ap-nea? What is wrong with my husband?????

An illness in a family affects everyone in the household, including the children. Although they did not talk about it much to either of us, I know it affected them too. I posted a note in my Bible that said: "It is not in trying, but in trusting . . . not in running, but in resting . . . not in wandering, but in praying . . .that we find the strength of the Lord."

I got the courage to tuck little scripture verses of hope into the frame of my husband's bathroom mirror:

When you pass through the waters, I will be with you; and when you pass through the rivers, they will not sweep over you. [O, God, you are with me!] When you walk through the fire, you will not be burned; the flames will not set you ablaze. For I am the LORD, your God, . . . your Savior.
—ISAIAH 43:2–3

I was driven to God. He was my only stay in all of those years of trouble. My husband kept telling me, "I am sick and tired of being sick and tired."

I asked myself, *Why must he blame me?* One of his relatives came to visit, and they both blamed me. He realized what he was doing but it was so easy to put the blame on me during those confusing days. I saved a letter he wrote to me in 1993. Here is part of it:

My Dear Barbara,
I really don't know where to start? I feel like a real jerk for treating you so harshly. I say a lot of things that are untrue and unnecessary. I understand how difficult this is for you as well as for me. I was clearly out of control and ask for your forgiveness. How can you have any feelings for me anymore? I don't under-stand. Some of the pressures of life have crowded out the essentials of our rela-tionship. I am deeply sorry for all the pain and frustration I have caused you! I do want you to be first in my life, the object of my love and my affection. I know

I have hurt you deeply and may never gain your respect and trust again. Please help me win your respect.

> *Love,*
> *your husband*

I found some rich verses in Isaiah chapter 38:

In the prime of my life must I go through the gates of death and be robbed of the rest of my years?

—verse 10

You restored me to health and let me live.

—verse 16

Surely it was for my benefit that I suffered such anguish. In your love you kept me from the pit of destruction; you have put all my sins behind your back.

—verse 17

The more I read, the more hope I got and the closer to God I was drawn. One particular verse spoke so deeply to my spirit that it is still tucked by a picture in his bathroom, the ink now faded: "Even when we are too weak to have any faith left, He remains faithful to us and will help us. He cannot disown us who are part of Himself and He will always carry out His promise to us" (2 Timothy 2:13, paraphrase).

OK, God, I prayed, *help me help my husband. He is too weak. We have found little hope from the doctors, but we need hope from You!*

I began reading—or rather, devouring—books, magazine articles, newspapers, medical reference books, anything that could or would help us both. I read about everything from diet to exercise, to chronic fatigue, to stress. He also began seeing a counselor.

The Answers

In December of 1993, my husband went to a holistic doctor and we finally got some answers in early 1994. Not only did my husband have diverticulitis, he also had irritable bowel syndrome. Plus, tests showed that he had been exposed to the Epstein-Barr virus and had other medical complications as well. He also had seven times the normal amount of yeast in his intestinal tract.

In my reading, I was finding all kinds of information about how to manage stress and some of the things from which my husband was suffering. In order to control stress, you have to learn how to recognize it, then educate yourself in how to combat it. The main ways to combat stress are to get enough rest and exercise, and eat healthy—lots of vegetables and less sugar since sugar feeds the yeast in the intestinal tract and was causing my husband's bloated feeling and weight gain.

I also found that the immune system is weakened by repeated use of antibiotic drugs. He had been prescribed those several times. They can cause toxins in the intestinal tract that can cause chronic problems in the entire digestive system. Chronic stress, along with chronic fatigue, further weakens the body's immune system, causing susceptibility to infection, depression, anxiety, insomnia, fatigue, viruses, neck and back pain, and other stress-related disorders. Unfortunately, a person who is over-worked, over-tired or driven tends to speed up and work even harder and faster, instead of slowing down. Minimizing the importance of stress is guaranteed to make it worse.

Chronic Fatigue Syndrome (CFS), which my husband had, was the disease of the 90s. It is linked to the Epstein-Barr and other viruses that cause exhaustion, aching joints, mental distortion, fatigue, physical problems, prostate pain, hair loss, memory loss, depression, panic, stress, emotional lows, headaches, sleep disturbance, weight gain, and on and on and on.

The more I read about my husband's diagnosis, the more I understood that stress can kill. One dear couple from our church saw how frustrated and weary we both had become and actually quit their Bible study with others to begin meeting weekly with us to listen, pray and encourage us. We will never forget that sacrificial love you gave us, Dave and JoAnne! Thank you!

One of the other things I found in my reading was that the older we get, the more physical exercise we need. My husband and I began walking together and lost weight.

> Physical training is of some value, but godliness [spiritual exercise] has value for all things, holding promise for both the present life and the life to come.
>
> —1 TIMOTHY 4:8

My Issues

I also began attending a Christian twelve-step group. Although I didn't get to the core of the sexual abuse, the group helped me begin to unearth the pot of memories that had been buried for so long. The deeper I got with God, the less I tried to control others. Abuse victims don't mean to control, but because a piece of their lives is so out of control, they subconsciously try to control everything and everyone. I had to realize that the only person I can control is myself. Trying to control others simply drives loved ones further away. God had to change me first!

I love how Damaris Carbaugh puts it:

> **In ourselves we may see hardened ground,**
> **empty spaces that long to be filled;**
> **But God sees our heart,**
> **and if we let Him start,**
> **an image of Christ He will build.**

As I allowed God to change me, the results were amazing. I began to trust myself and God more. He was beginning to chip away at those rough places, to bring out the image of Christ in me.

We are God's workmanship, created in Christ Jesus.
—EPHESIANS 2:10

Richard A. Swenson, M.D., quoted in *More Than Meets the Eye* says, "Finally at long last, God will deliver us from our dimness, and in the shelter of the Most High we will enter our rest!"

It was good to know that God cared about us just the way we were. He had a wonderful purpose in what we had faced. Even in the midst of our conflict and discouragement, He was faithful to us.

Stretching the Soul

God never allows a person to run for Him or with Him who hasn't been stretched in his or her thinking or faith, or in the ability to live or to love. Sometimes our souls hit a wall and no amount of strength or pressing will move the problem. It is this challenge to our souls that stretches them, enabling us to face situations we think are impossible or things we can't endure. I have faced more soul stretches in my lifetime than I want to admit. God got me through every single one of them and will probably get me through several more.

We must live above our circumstances—even in the middle of them—in order to be victorious, and only God does that with us. In the midst of the conflict and discouragement with our marriage, my abuse, the betrayals, and my husband's physical problems, the perplexities were stretching our souls. God wanted to stretch us back to Himself.

But times like these are not easy to face. We are disappointed and become discouraged with our lives, or our mundane marriages, or our partners. And we feel powerless and hopeless when we can't see our way clear. It is then, and only then, that we need to see Jesus, come to Him and be like Him. As we run to Him with the enthusiasm of a child running after a butterfly, He meets our deepest need.

I don't know how God got me through all of this, but He did. I had to do my part in the letting-go process. That was so hard for me, the person who liked to be in control of things. But when I let go and let God, I realized I needed to go deeper with Him, and Him alone. That was when I realized that only God sees deeply into our souls. It is through this—a truly near-death experience—that we walk in the valley of the shadow of death where we see no evil and know that He is with us.

I know our spouses walk at different levels of spiritual and emotional health than we do. Because each of us is raised differently, we bring all kinds of stuff into our marriage. Since I was raised by a wonderful minister daddy who led our home spiritually, I think my husband felt pressure from me to be on a pedestal of some kind. God had to teach me that I demanded more of my husband than he had been designed by God to give. That communicated to him that I thought he could never measure up.

My faith took a deeper turn when I let go and let God to do what I could not do. He enabled me to face a situation that I thought was impossible. I felt like I couldn't go on or endure for a single moment more. But God got me through every single circumstance, and I can now look back and see that the stretching strengthened my faith.

Retrouvaille

One way that happened was when I came upon a miracle that helped our marriage get back in tune with God. In the July 1996 issue of *Focus on the Family* magazine, I read about Retrouvaille, a program for couples whose marriages are in crisis because of alcoholism, adultery and other destructive habits or addictions. It was more intense than the Marriage Encounter program, which is designed more for people whose marriages simply need a tune-up. For the first time it appeared there was a program and people who could help us reconnect with one another. I knew we had to attend.

Churches, in many ways, have failed couples like us who face severe marriage problems. Although there are many books to read and pastors to counsel, if the authors or pastors do not understand what sexual abuse and infidelity do to damage a life or marriage, they can be of little help. They must first educate themselves about the devastation that sexual abuse and infidelity cause in a person and a marriage relationship.

In learning about abuse, I have been able climb out of the darkness and help others climb out too. As I continue to find answers for myself and our marriage, I have been able to help not only myself but also our marriage and other marriages as well.

The second miracle was that I actually picked up the phone and called Retrouvaille to say that my husband and I needed to be there. Just like a drug addict or alcoholic who says he wants to come clean has to pick up the phone and call a counselor or detox facility, I had to make that phone call. Picking up the phone was the hard part.

Victims are good at hiding, at isolating themselves, at not dealing with themselves or their stuff. The "not knowing" is sometimes more frightening than the knowing. And in the not dealing with—the not coming clean—we remain as ignorant and as fearful as those who are lying in their vomit in the streets. I knew I needed cleaning up.

When I dialed the number for Retrouvaille—1-800-470-2230—I was shocked to hear they were hosting a weekend near us within just a few weeks.

I took the magazine to our pastor and showed him. He said, "The church will pay half for you and your husband to go. Come back and tell me what you learned." That was a confirmation we should go. After I showed the article to my husband and told him the church would help financially, he agreed to go.

The third miracle was that we actually attended a Retrouvaille Weekend, which was a lifeline for our very troubled marriage.

Retrouvaille, pronounced re·trô·vî´, is a French word that means rediscovery. It was one of the most valuable tools we discovered to help salvage our marriage. It was a re-beginning for us.

Retrouvaille

For you have delivered me from death and my feet from stumbling that I may walk before God in the light of life.

—Psalm 56:13

For this reason a man will leave his father and his mother and be united to his wife, and they will become one flesh.

—Genesis 2:24

This has been God's definition of marriage from the beginning of time:

One + One = One
One Man + One Woman = God's covenant relationship with Him

The Retrouvaille Experience

Although Retrouvaille is not advertised as a fix-all, their statistics show that eighty percent of the couples who attend have been able to rebuild their marriages. It is simply a tool to help marriage partners communicate more effectively with each other. For us, it was a new beginning after much darkness and pain.

We attended Retrouvaille in September 1996. It was an experience we will never forget and we came away with principles we know work.

Retrouvaille is Catholic in origin, but is open to all couples regardless of their religious background, their current affiliation, or lack thereof. (The organization has since added a Protestant program) The Retrouvaille program is similar to Marriage Encounter—with one important difference: It is designed for crisis marriages. (That was ours for sure!) The leaders are couples whose own marriages once nearly failed. They share how they overcame adultery, alcoholism, etc., and inspire couples in hurting marriages to try new ways to love one another. The entire program is Christ-centered.

As we entered the hotel, we noticed how distant some of the other thirty-five couples were toward each other. It was very obvious some did not want to be there, and in some cases you could almost cut the anger with a knife. Most couples were not smiling and, as far as I could see, my husband and I were the only ones holding hands.

Maybe our marriage isn't as bad as it seems, I thought to myself. We later learned that some of the couples at the weekend were already divorced or separated. Others were newlyweds or had been married only a couple of years and had been given this wonderful gift by their parents or in-laws as a learning tool or preventative weekend.

The Weekend

A typical Retrouvaille Weekend is held in a hotel or retreat facility. You are pretty much "locked down" for an intense weekend together—no television, no clocks, watches or other distractions. Three married couples (leaders, not participants) begin by sharing their painful stories of disillusionment, anger and conflict (some very much like ours). First the husband tells his version of their story and then the wife has five minutes to tell it from her perspective.

At our weekend, a priest also shared his story of growing up in an alcoholic home and how that deeply affected him and shoved him into anger.

There were boxes of Kleenex placed all over the conference room. It wasn't long before emotions and memories of deep pain, mistrust, betrayal and anger began to surface. Emotions and tears came easily to most of the women, but it wasn't long before several of the men, including my spouse, were wiping away their tears as well.

Each of us was given a journal and a pen. The instructions were to dig layer by layer into the core of our feelings. The leaders showed us techniques to get beyond the surface feelings, below the anger, deeper than the he/she needs in order to understand why we react the way we do. The process was likened to peeling an onion, layer by layer, until you get to the core of what you really feel and why.

Writing the Answers

Then we were given key questions to answer in our journals. What we wrote would later become our dialog with one another.

The leaders reminded us that no one has the right to tell another person how to feel and that feelings are neither right nor wrong. You feel a certain way about what was done to you or what was said or how your spouse reacted to the situation. They encouraged us to write how we felt about the questions themselves, and we were told to rate how we felt about our answers on a scale of one to ten.

We were instructed not to use the truth like a club by blaming or trying to change our partner since the only person you can change is yourself. (Boy, did I already know that! The more I talked about what I wanted, the less it happened, and the more out of control our home had become)

The husbands were then dismissed to their individual rooms while the wives scattered throughout the main meeting room. That gave each of us quality, alone time with no distractions to quietly answer the questions. We were given a time limit, ranging from ten minutes to an hour, to answer each question. If we ran out of things to write during those timeframes, the leaders told us just to keep writing, assuring us that the heart and emotions would follow.

This was not going to be easy after decades of pain and denial!

But I never ran out of things to write because I was used to journaling and it was natural for me to write and express my emotions. However, it was a new experience for my husband and new for us as a couple. Although it was not that easy for my husband, write we did. We had no choice!

We wrote forty-seven pages to one another that weekend! Ever since learning about this valuable tool of communication, we continue to write to one another to express our feelings.

After the time of writing, each wife was to go to the room where her husband was and, without talking, exchange the letters both had written in their journals. We were given a certain timeframe to read each other's letters. We were told to read them without any discussion or verbal exchange whatsoever. That was to make certain there were no arguments, bad talk or fights. We were told to read what the other had written twice—once with our heads (to understand it intellectually) and again with our hearts (to put ourselves in the other person's shoes to feel what they are feeling).

No one counseled us, and there were no exchanges with the presenting couples unless you got stuck or needed advice on how to proceed with the writing assignments. They made it clear they were couples just like us—real people with real problems with real people—who had gotten past the anger, pain and hurt and have healed.

They taught us that when you have an argument or disagreement, it's best to take a step back to get away from the anger and write down what you are feeling. "Do not judge," we were told, "but tell the other person how he or she makes you feel." Because feelings are neither right nor wrong (you have a right to your feelings), dialog is a safe place to go to validate your feelings about a certain problem. Even if we may not understand or accept those feelings, we can share who we are with our spouse.

My Dilemma of Discouragement

I was pouring myself out to my husband. But after the first day and a half, I wanted to go home. He was not understanding me at all! With his engineer's mindset, he was trying to analyze, instead of understand, my true feelings. I was pouring my heart out to him with real honesty—more than I had done in a long, long time. I was willing to risk being vulnerable to him, but he still was trying to change me, to fix me. (After all, he fixed problems at work, didn't he?) He wanted me to go talk to the couples who were not counselors. That made me feel sad, uncertain, and doubtful that this whole thing was even worth it at all.

In one session, we were asked to rate on a scale of one to ten how we were feeling and what color or image we'd use to describe our feelings. I said, "I am feeling lonely, sad and scared. If a low is a ten, I would give it a nine. The color I am feeling is gray because I feel like I am looking dimly as through a cloudy glass at a rain cloud that is ready to burst. The image is of a door that is partially open or partially shut."

A Breakthrough

We had a lot of work to do on our marriage, and I prayed God would break in. He did!

We were asked to answer the question, "What are my reasons for wanting to go on living?" and were encouraged to write until we could write no more and then keep on writing. This was a turning point in our weekend together.

I had seen the tears come to the surface of my husband's eyes when one of the presenting couples was sharing. In my letter to him in answer to the above question, I shared how I had been touched by his tears. "What were you feeling right then?" I asked in my letter. I told him that I need to see his tender, caring side and that those tears were not a sign of weakness but of strength.

I told him it takes a real man to be able to cry. "I want to see the real you when you are hurting, when you need me just to listen or hold you or wipe away the tears." I reminded him that he had gone through some deep emotional pain that I had never experienced—pain that I would never fully understand or could even begin to try to. I reminded him that through the pain, deep valleys, low water and great troubles we all go through, we are not alone. I encouraged him that since we had started to reconnect with one another, we should continue to write to one another—"to get the pain out and verbalize it on paper because this would bring a new, healthier you."

God broke into our marriage at the very end of Retrouvaille when I thought there was no hope! At this session I read what my husband had written to me as his reasons for wanting to go on living.

Here is a portion of what he wrote:

My Dear Barbara,

How could I have been so blind to have ignored this precious way of communicating with you? You were much quicker to see and use this valuable means of communication, and I marvel at your wisdom and understanding.

There have been many reasons I have not wanted to go on living: the way the world is, my own personal impaired health, betrayal on my job, politics and a lack of fulfillment. Our marriage gave me the desire to "tune out" life, society and you. That only caused me to dull the pain, and fortunately I didn't "act on it" as my father did. Our friend JoAnne calls it, "the dark night of the soul," but perhaps for me it is a wake-up call! I have begun to see the pain and sufferings that my own dear father must have experienced to cause him to want to end his life. I would have loved to share family gatherings, our sons, different things with my dad that I never got a chance to share. Your dad has been wonderful in filling that void, but it is still not my dad. . . .

I have to stop here because this is when my husband started weeping as I have never seen him weep before. God broke deep inside our marriage when my husband began to see as a blessing the "curse" that had once been destructive in his own life, his work, our families, and our marriage.

When the LORD brought back the captives to Zion, we were like men who dreamed [were restored to health]. Our mouths were filled with laughter, our tongues with songs of joy. Then it was said among the nations, "The LORD has done great things for them." . . . Those who sow in tears will reap with songs of joy. He who goes out weeping, carrying seed to sow, will return with songs of joy, carrying sheaves with him.

—PSALM 126:1,2,5,6

My *New International Version Recovery Devotional Bible* says in the meditation from this psalm that "when we who were captive found freedom and began to enjoy the fruit of recovery, it was a dream come true. After tears of guilt, shame, repentance and grief were shed, laughter began to be part of life again. Just like the tears, laughter does good like a medicine. The Lord has done great things for us and when we are truly aware of how much He has done, songs of joy will come naturally."

After the Weekend

Because the hurt and pain of falling out of love cannot be healed in a single Retrouvaille weekend experience, a follow-up series of presentations provides a time and place to work on the couples' marriage relationships. Several topics are explored during these sessions, among them: Beginning Again, Love Is a Decision, Forgiveness, A Look at Me.

Post Script

For more information about Retrouvaille, go to www.retrouvaille.org or call 1-800-470-2230.

AFTERTHOUGHT

From my journal—summer 2002

Last evening I was consumed with a tenderness and love for my husband that has not been there with that intensity in a long, long time. I have always loved him deeply and knew I could never break our marriage vows and leave him when the pain was so raw. I think it has taken me this many years to grieve all the losses that I have had in my life, and maybe I am just beginning to grieve the loss I experienced from his betrayals. During a very intimate moment, I began wailing and weeping when I should have been high with joy.

He could not understand my deep soul cry of emotional pain and just held me close and wiped away my tears. "How could I have been such a jerk?" he asked. That kind of tenderness and compassion was new to me.

In between the sobs, I tried to explain what was happening to me. I told him that I believe I am just now beginning to experience the deep, enveloping grief that spills so freely out of my soul damage, damage not only from what he did, but also from how others have treated and abused me.

We are beginning to understand one another at a different level and talk about things that have never been talked about. I have even empathized with him about how difficult it must have been for him to live with the web of deceit created by the affairs. I truly want to understand my husband and want us both to be able to talk with one another about anything. I think he is finally beginning to realize all the losses that we have both had and has come to an *acceptance of the fact that what happened cannot be changed. The only things we can both change are ourselves and the way we treat each other.*

For the first time, I am able to look at the pain—his and mine—with different eyes. I see now, not from my wounded spirit, but from my whole spirit. And those tears come from the grief that has truly never come until recently. That grief is so wonderfully resurrecting my spirit both to my husband and to God's Spirit. For the first time my husband and I are working together and not against one another.

For the first time I feel I have a soul mate. For the first time I know we can jump any hurdle because God is truly working deeply in both of us when we work together to serve one another and His kingdom.

Post Script

Jesus, "who for the joy set before him, endured the cross" (Hebrews 12:2), and the result was the finished work that provided salvation. I feel like I have endured much, and I can say with Joseph: "You intended to harm me, but God intended it for good to accomplish what is now being done, the saving of many lives" (Genesis 50:20).

PREPARATION
FOR THE CALL

I was very troubled during a particular night in January of 1996. God finally woke me up "as a man wakes from the stupor of wine" (Psalm 78:65).

Not knowing why I was so troubled, I obeyed the Holy Spirit's prompting and went to my Bible. I opened it to Isaiah 61. I began to pray fervently for my household, including the ex-con who was detoxing (coming off heroin, crack cocaine and alcohol addiction) and living with us while he waited for a bed in a drug rehab program to become available.

I did not know until morning that at the same time I was awakened in the night, he had been very frightened by demons calling out his name. But during that time, I was inspired through God's Word as He was already beginning to reveal His call on my life while I meditated on and paraphrased Isaiah 61 verse by verse.

New International Version (NIV)

1. "The Spirit of the Sovereign LORD is on me, because the LORD has anointed me to preach good news to the poor. He has sent me to bind up the brokenhearted, to proclaim freedom for the captives and release from darkness for the prisoners,"

Inspired by God's Holy Spirit

1. The Spirit of God has called me to do the work of an evangelist. He has given me hope to pour His healing into the poor in spirit. We must be possessed by Him! The purpose of my existence is to offer recovery of sight from spiritual darkness and freedom in Christ.

2. "to proclaim the year of the LORD's favor and the day of vengeance of our God, to comfort all who mourn,"

2. God, grant us Your favor as we learn that You are always near to us when others have failed us! We need each other for comfort and encouragement.

3. "and provide for those who grieve in Zion—to bestow on them a crown of beauty instead of ashes, the oil of gladness instead of mourning, and a garment of praise instead of a spirit of despair. They will be called oaks of righteousness, a planting of the LORD for the display of his splendor."

3. God will wipe away all our tears! We are worthy because He delights in us! A crown is ours because we are children of a King! He gives our countenance a smile, joy instead of sadness and death, which brings praise as we worship Him! We are no longer homeless or worthless! God makes us strong in Christ because He is the Vine, we are the branches (John 15), and we need to be deeply connected to Him to grow with deep roots in Him, giving us hope and trust for our future!

4. "They will rebuild the ancient ruins and restore the places long devastated; they will renew the ruined cities that have been devastated for generations."

4. This builds strong character to replace what the locusts have stolen as we surrender our will to His. Resurrection comes from death, restoring to me the God of my salvation and the salvation of my family as I pray that the generational curse be reversed and healed through Christ!

5. "Aliens will shepherd your flocks; foreigners will work your fields and vineyards."

5. God gives us close friends who are like family to love us as God loves us.

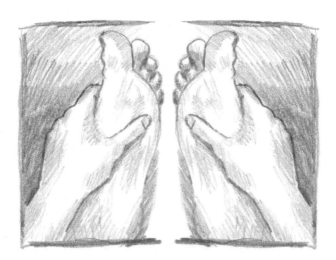

6. "And you will be called priests of the LORD, and you will be named ministers of our God. You will feed on the wealth of nations and in their riches you will boast."

6. And you will be God's anointed son or daughter and will be given a new name, proclaiming what He has done! We become Jesus' hands and feet as He blesses us with spiritual and emotional abundance and wealth!

7. "Instead of their shame my people will receive a double portion, and instead of disgrace they will rejoice in their inheritance; and so they will inherit a double portion in their land, and everlasting joy will be theirs."

7. You are no longer defeated with guilt; you are an adopted son or daughter who no longer thinks poorly of yourself. God will give much to you as you come out of the darkness into His light. Your joy will overflow and run over!

8. "For I, the LORD, love justice; I hate robbery and iniquity. In my faithfulness I will reward them and make an everlasting covenant with them."

8. God seeks an honest heart after righteousness because you have been saved from your old life of sin! He rewards us and gave of His own shed blood because He deeply loves us and calls us to Himself!

9. "Their descendants will be known among the nations and their offspring among the peoples. All who see them will acknowledge that they are a people the LORD has blessed."

9. God promises to bless our offspring as others realize what God has done in our lives. This is a testimony of His power in our lives.

10. "I delight greatly in the LORD; my soul rejoices in my God. For he has clothed me with garments of salvation and arrayed me in a robe of righteousness, as a bridegroom adorns his head like a priest, and as a bride adorns herself with her jewels."

10. God desires happy, joyful living as our souls are freed from death and brought back to life! Peace and hope flood my soul as God brings deliverance from bondage that I never had before! The old is shed and new life in Christ put on as I ready myself for His return as a bride does for her husband. Our lives sparkle with peace, life, happiness and joy unspeakable!

11. "For as the soil makes the sprout come up and a garden causes seeds to grow, so the Sovereign LORD will make righteousness and praise spring up before all nations."

11. For as the message of salvation takes deep root in the soil (Matthew 13:18–23), God brings beauty out of ashes. Our lives take a new direction and flower and grow. As we share our faith with others, He produces joy no one can take away (John 16:22).

It is always after a failure that man does his greatest work for God!

—DAVE WILKERSON

THE CALL
BY GOD

I will keep you and will make you to be a covenant for the people, to restore the land and to reassign its desolate inheritances, to say to the captives, "Come out," and to those in darkness, "Be free!"

—Isaiah 49:8–9

Then will the eyes of the blind be opened, and the ears of the deaf unstopped. Then will the lame leap like a deer.

—Isaiah 35:5–6

Diamonds in the Rough

We are all diamonds in the rough, created by an almighty loving Father who has a divine purpose for each of us. In their natural state, diamonds are covered in dirt. Some of us have more dirt in our lives than others. But when God removes that dirt, our inner beauty is revealed.

God calls each of us to something, a ministry where He can use the gifts He gives us. Allowing Him to use us in this way involves a commitment to God and to one another. The ministry I have is not mine; it is His. They are not my gifts; they are His. He has given me His tears on my face and His hurt in my heart for the most wounded broken people I know. I have been called to minister in prisons and crack houses. Even drug dealers in these places have invited me to share my personal faith with them.

New Eyes

In 1996, we had gone into a minimum-security prison with friends from our Bible study group who had made the arrangements. That experience was completely foreign to us. We were given the name of an inmate who at the time was a new Christian. He kept us on our toes when he asked us to tell him what we were learning in our own quiet time with God and in our church. It was the spontaneity of *his ministering to us* that drew us back inside the prison. We realized that we needed to be serious about God if we were going to be able minister to him.

As God gave us new eyes—Jesus' eyes—my husband and I began to see people who were blind, not physically but spiritually. We began to see the spiritually lame and crippled—crack and heroin addicts, alcoholics, pimps, victims, broken, hurting people—as Jesus sees them, and they gave *us* a gift. They reflected back to us who we are without God. They taught us to widen our hearts to every living creature, a revelation more precious than any scripture.

Now, instead of having negative emotions toward the poor, our hearts were opened with a compassion that brought a release in our spirits. We had a new desire to actually seek out the company of the blind, the lame and the crippled because they gave us a gift by revealing to us our inner selves in which we hardly recognized the people we once were. (See Luke 14:12–14)

I found myself actually *seeking out* the company of the crack addicts as I began to realize I was as messed up as they were! When I put myself on their level, like Jesus did with the woman at the well in John 4, they began to listen to me. I easily shared my brokenness with them and walked alongside them with a new understanding. I no longer desired the superficial friends I at one time had.

> "Before I formed you in the womb I knew you, before you were born I set you apart; I appointed you a prophet to the nations. . . . You must go to everyone I send you to and say whatever I command you. Do not be afraid of them, for I am with you and I will rescue you," declares the LORD.
> —JEREMIAH 1:5,7–8

Friends who knew about our ministry in the prisons gave us names of hardened criminals, gang members, prostitutes and Boston-area gangsters. Members of the Christian Motorcyclists Association chapter to which we belonged because of my husband's love of cycling also passed along names to us. Many with whom we shared the love of Jesus over a cup of coffee or meals at our home prayed to receive Him personally into their hearts and lives. This brought much inner peace and joy to us because we knew it brought an inner peace and joy to those who had never been given hope before.

But there were others who criticized us, much as the religious leaders faulted Jesus in Luke 15:1–2: "This man welcomes sinners and eats with them."

I wanted to be what a friend calls "Jesus with skin on" to these people and live out before them what Oswald Chambers alludes to in *Still Higher for His Highest*:

To picture Jesus Christ as One who sits down beside the brokenhearted [to sympathize], is not only thoroughly to misunderstand our Lord, but to prevent Him from doing what He came to do. He does come to the broken-hearted, to the captives bound by a cursed hereditary tendency, to the blind who grope for light, to the man bruised and crushed by his surroundings, but he does not come as a sympathizer. He "binds up the brokenhearted, gives release to the captives, recovering of sight to the blind; He sets at liberty them that are bruised" (Luke 4:18). Jesus Christ is not a mere sym-pathizer, He is a Savior, and the only One.

A Time to Think

God's call in my life to ministry came before I knew how much it would cost me. The cost of my time and our actual financial outlay as I gave of myself, away from our family to "do unto others" came at a price. In listen-ing to God's still, small voice from His Spirit to mine, He told me to trust Him. All that was expected of me was my complete obedience to His call and my dependence on His leading.

By early 1999, our two older sons had married and our youngest had moved into an apartment with Christian roommates before he got married. It gave me more time to myself to think and work on getting better. There was really no choice. I just had to get better—or stay in denial, and I didn't want to be there anymore! I refused to be destroyed by my past any longer, but I had to be quiet before God and listen to the voice of His Spirit speaking to my spirit, knowing that He would heal me.

Life began to begin to be good again as I started dealing with all the trauma that had been dealt to me. Memory after memory, layer upon layer, pot after pot was uncovered, just as David Seamands, the conference speaker in 1985, had said would happen. Memories flooded in as I had more time to think about my life. It was time finally to take care of me!

I consciously made up my mind at that time that I had no other choice than to put God first. Everything else would have to be in second place. Everything else—all distractions, all other voices that were not a priority—had to go!

During this time of solitude and sabbatical from all other distractions, I spent large parts of quiet time with Him in the aloneness of our home. Instead of isolating myself there as I had done before, I spent the time in prayer and in the Word as God prepared me for His call.

Early on in this time of solitude was when I told my husband that I needed to find out why I was born.

His response had been that I was a wonderful wife and mother.

"No," I said. "It's much deeper than you or I even understand!" I knew that as I prayed and waited on God, He would reveal it to me.

> Then the LORD reached out his hand and touched my mouth and said to me, "Now, I have put my words in your mouth [and] . . . I will make my words in your mouth a fire."
>
> —JEREMIAH 1:9; 5:14

My Call to Ministry

I was just beginning to understand my true identity based on scripture. God was fanning the flame and encouraging the hidden gifts deep inside me that could not stay hidden any longer!

When God began to reveal His specific call to me in 1999, others questioned it. Prior to this time, I had gone through a support program for victims of abuse. As I worked on my issues and my healing over a two-year period, I began to realize that I could use what I had learned to help others.

But I was told by a person who in my mind was in a position of spiritual authority that I could not minister in this way within the organized church. If I wanted to do this with the blessing of the church, he wanted me to document every phone call and every person that God brought to my door or that I met out on the streets.

He went on to say, "You're not healthy enough to do this!" My emotional state and spiritual gifts were being questioned. (In retrospect, I think that what this person said was a form of spiritual abuse) My mind, with its ingrained performance-based behavior pattern, screamed, *Something's wrong with me!*

I gently reminded myself that God accepts me just the way I am. God is the one who encourages who we are. Conversely, it is man who makes the rules, or the law, that somehow make me have to prove myself worthy of the calling.

I was angry about how this person wanted me to do this kind of ministry to "the least of these," but my husband was even angrier! "How can they treat you like this?" he fumed. I submitted with humility for three months and allowed the church to assign a mentor to me. Eventually, though, I had enough. It drove me outside the church into the streets where I felt called and more comfortable anyway.

(The "blind, the deaf and the crippled" label from Isaiah 35:5–6 can also apply to those in the church who are indifferent and uncaring, unsympathetic and not knowledgeable about the problems and the needs these people face. Not seeing these people as Jesus sees them inhibits a person's ability to understand how to help them recover from these destructive patterns)

My reaction reminds me of a couplet quoted by Jan Karon in *In This Mountain* and attributed simply to "an English missionary":

> **Some want to live within the sound**
> **of church and chapel bell,**
> **I want to run a rescue shop within a yard of hell.**

Validation

But Ruth, my mentor for those three months, was a gift from God. She was a wonderful woman from my church who understood me. In fact those three months have now turned into three years (and counting) of her faithfulness in word and prayer for me. Since she was my mentor, I had to give her written documentation of all those people God was sending to me. During that time she validated my call, the purpose for my existence, and my spiritual gifts, including the gift of mercy, which I didn't even know I had.

In answer to my questions about why I was able to reach out to so many people, she replied: "Barb, it's because you have the gift few people have, the gift of mercy. I wish the church was full of people just like you! Very few could do effectively what God has called you to do. Continue to go outside the church, and don't question your ability!"

My husband and I continued to get the names of people who were hardened criminals, gang members, prostitutes and Boston-area gangsters who we led to personal faith in Christ. Most Christians wouldn't dream of talking to what Jesus calls "the least of these," but these are the ones who need Him the most!

I now realize as I look back at the restrictions under which I was required to minister that it was all for a purpose. In all the writing and documentation I was required to do, I was actually beginning to write this book—and maybe subsequent ones!

When we don't understand who we are in Christ, we will do what we think others expect of us in order to gain their approval. You will never be satisfied or know God's call on your life that way. The approval of people is usually conditional and always temporary. God's approval is everlasting.

As I grew in my relationship to my Father, my perception of myself began to change. I understood for the first time in my life why God had put me on earth and what He had gifted me to do.

The prophet Jeremiah was instructed by God to call for women of God to cry out, weep and wail against the evil consequences of sin: "Call for the wailing women to come. . . . Let them come quickly and wail over us till our eyes overflow with tears and water streams from our eyelids" (Jeremiah 9:17–18). He asked them to come unashamedly, calling on Jehovah to see them through the darkness, and humbly as they consecrated themselves, with no concern what others might think about their doing what they were called by God to do.

As God changed my inner spirit, I began to be able to love and take care of myself again. I had always taken care of so many others. Now I was beginning to take care of me, and the Jesus inside me made me free to love, regardless of others' responses to or perception of me.

> **The place God calls you to is the place where the world's deep hunger and your deep gladness meet.**
> —FREDERICK BUECHNER

MAXIMUM SECURITY

I had been in and out of prison many times, but that day in 2000 was my first time in a maximum-security facility. As I drove up to the prison, it hit me with full force: *This is just like in the movies.* Only this was real!

Just seeing the tall, gray prison with the ugly, barbed wire that made sure no one got in and no one escaped brought deep, dark sadness to my spirit. Five long and painful years of ministering with Jesus' love and compassion to one of the guys who was now inside those walls hit me like a ton of bricks. Tears welled up in my eyes, and I thought to myself, *How in the world am I going to scrape together enough courage to go inside this place?*

But I knew I had to go. I had an appointment with the prison chaplain. Although we had never met, I felt like I already knew him because we had spoken by phone and exchanged several e-mails about the inmate to whom he was also ministering spiritually. It was a good meeting.

Getting Easier

When I drove up to the prison a few weeks later, I felt much stronger than on my first visit. I knew my husband and my friends were praying for me, and I sang praise songs all the way. I refused to be intimidated by the prison itself, by the guards or by not knowing what to expect. I knew I might be frisked or even strip-searched.

I reminded myself to remember my purpose for being there—my sense of mission and the call of God on my life. "I, even I, have spoken; yes, I have called [her]. I will bring [her], and [she] will succeed in [her] mission" (Isaiah 48:15). (I know the text uses male pronouns, but I needed to personalize this verse)

God had given me so many wonderful verses to claim for my life as well as for the lives in spiritual darkness to whom my husband and I were ministering. Many verses kept coming to my mind as I walked up the prison steps that day.

> I will keep you and will make you to be a covenant for the people, to restore the land and to reassign its desolate inheritances, to say to the captives, "Come out," and to those in darkness, "Be free!"
> —ISAIAH 49:8–9

> If I make my bed in hell, behold, thou art there.
> —PSALM 139:8 KJV

Suddenly God reminded me that He had actually called us to seek those who were making their beds in Hell. Wow, what a revelation! Only God could do a thing like that as He revealed His perfect will for me to be in this intense ministry.

> A man who strays from the path of understanding comes to rest in the company of the dead.
> —PROVERBS 21:16

That reminded me of *Dead Man Walking*, the movie about the Catholic nun who went into prisons to give hope and a cup of cold water in Jesus' name.

The verses that I had underlined in my Bible kept coming back:

> Praise be to the Lord, to God our Savior, who daily bears our burdens. Our God is a God who saves; from the Sovereign LORD comes escape from death.
> —PSALM 68:19–20

It seemed to me that being in prison must be just like death. But then I remembered my own denial and pain that had been a curse to my soul. Wasn't that a prison in itself—a death-like experience? What a miracle that God was using my husband and me to lead people from physical and spiritual death.

In the Lobby

When I pushed the prison door open, I was pleasantly surprised to be greeted by a little guy, probably all of three years old. It took me off guard for just a moment. He had what I thought was a pacifier in his mouth and looked at me with a great big grin. His wide eyes sparkled. What a gift to me when all I was expecting was stark coldness and iron, gray walls.

I saw his mommy, probably not older than eighteen, watching him from nearby to make sure he didn't slip through the doors into the cool summer evening outside. I found out later that his name was Isaiah and that he was there to visit his daddy. I wondered if Isaiah even knew that he was in a prison?

No place for an innocent child to be, I thought. *Maybe that's all he's known?* I asked myself.

Isaiah soon busied himself on the concrete floor, playing with what I had thought was his pacifier. It was actually a colored plastic top. Now that he had taken it out of his mouth, he was spinning it wildly on the floor.

Preparing to Visit

For a few minutes my thoughts were distracted by Isaiah until I remembered why I was there. I checked in at the visiting desk. The female guard remembered me from my visit a few weeks earlier. *How nice to be noticed in a place like this,* I thought. Then I realized she was just doing her job. She seemed to enjoy what she was doing as she joked with the visitors. Her laugh was welcomed.

I gave the guard my driver's license and deposited $20 in the account of our incarcerated friend so he could purchase snacks and toiletries from the canteen. The guard handed my license back along with a paper and matter-of-factly told me to return it to her after I filled it out completely. I put down our friend's name and his prison number, my name and address, my license number and registration, and my birth date. I marked "No" in all the blanks beside questions like: "Have you ever been convicted of a felony offense?" "Been arrested?" "Had any convictions?" *Who, me?* I thought. *I'm squeaky clean except for a speeding ticket I got about six years ago!*

As I sat down to wait, I noticed all the female visitors who were probably girlfriends, mothers, sisters, aunties, grandmothers or wives. Our prisoner friend calls me "Mom" because I have been like a spiritual mother to him since my husband and I had started ministering to him in a minimum-security prison five years ago. I remember being shocked when he called me "Ma," but at the same time it felt like a privilege to have him call me that. He put me on his visiting list as his mother. I wondered if his birth mother was even on his list, or if she had ever come to visit him. I had met her several times at our home and in his sister's church.

The guard interrupted my thoughts when she called me. She came out of the glass booth where she had been sitting and told me to put everything I had brought in with me in a locker. She motioned to a row of pay lockers like you'd find in a gym. I asked if I could take my Bible with me, but she said, "No, you must take everything out of your pockets, including paper and Kleenex. Take off all your jewelry, including your earrings, and remove your hair clip and your belt." I felt slightly intimidated, wondering what would come next. I did as she had instructed, hoping my jeans would stay up when I removed my belt. I put it and the other items in the locker with my Bible, but I couldn't figure out how to put the quarter in or take the key out.

Everyone must be watching me, I thought. They were. I was mortified! There must have been about thirty-five people in the lobby. Suddenly I heard myself saying to no one in particular: "How do I get my quarter in the machine and remove my key?" A compassionate lady helped me. I put the money in, removed the key and sat down next to her.

Talking to Debbie

I had prayed before entering the prison that God would use me boldly. The helpful woman and I introduced ourselves to each other. Her name was Debbie and she was visiting her brother who was in for a fourth offense for drunk driving. She noticed that I had forgotten to take off my wedding rings.

Oops, I thought. *I've got to spend another quarter!* In went the rings. I closed the locker, took the key out and sat back down to resume our conversation. I began my story of how we met the inmate I was visiting several years ago. I told her how I had become very involved with his whole family, including his unwed, pregnant sister who had been a drug addict and dancer/ stripper. I told Debbie how I had shared my faith with her, leading her to Christ the day after a Jehovah's Witness lady had come to her door.

Another lady was watching us. She motioned to me, telling me to remove my wristwatch. "Can't I just pull my long-sleeved shirt down so the guard couldn't see it?" I asked her.

"No, everything must come off or they won't let you in," she responded.

I started to laugh. Another quarter. *Wow, this is really like in the movies!* Off came the watch. I closed the locker again and sat down to continue my conversation with Debbie. I told her how I had shared my testimony the previous week on J-Light Christian Radio in Framingham, Massachusetts, and how my husband and I had gotten calls from drug dealers to share our faith in crack houses.

Debbie listened intently and told me she hoped her brother would make it, but she was doubtful he would. She told me how much she loved him but that the family had all but given up on him. I told her I would be praying for her and for her brother too.

She told me he had never been the same after his grandfather who raised him died. Her brother was only eight at the time, and she agreed with me that he probably had never grieved the grandfather's death. I could certainly relate because of my own experience. Since I hadn't recognized or grieved the loss of my childhood innocence that was stolen from me, I knew what it was like to be stuck in grief.

I told her that everyone has a God-shaped hole that only God can fill and that our root issues from our childhood must be faced and dealt with, or the pain and denial will crop up like a poison again and again. I told her that our anger must be recognized and faced, or it will destroy us. The anger turns either outward to hurt others or inward into denial that hurts us.

It was so strange to share so intimately with a complete stranger. I was intrigued by how easily God enabled me to do so. I realized how spiritually hungry this woman was and how much the Holy Spirit had taught me as I healed from my own painful experiences. He had uniquely equipped me to minister to those dealing with other deep-seated issues in their lives.

Going In

"Sixteen," the guard yelled.

"What's that mean?" I asked Debbie.

"Hurry up, let's get in line. We were here first," she said. "They only let sixteen in at a time. The others have to wait until our hour is over." They herded us into line like cattle.

Each visitor had to pass through the metal detectors one by one. Some had not listened to the guard earlier and had to remove everything from their hair and put the clips, ponytail holders, etc. in their lockers.

Debbie noticed a lady wearing sandals and said, "She won't get in. They don't allow sandals here."

I was glad I had worn shoes. It felt like I was in a concentration-type camp and was getting quite nervous because I didn't know what to expect once I got on the other side of the detector. I thanked God for giving me Debbie as a guardian angel to walk by my side that evening. I was not alone.

I remembered my life's verse: "I can do all things through Christ who strengthens me" (Philippians 4:13 NKJV). I knew I could not go through this experience without relying completely on God's strength, not my own.

When it was my turn, I walked through the detector, hoping the alarm wouldn't sound. I had indeed followed the rules—even though it had cost me a few quarters.

"When it's your turn, put your license on the table, take off your shoes and go inside the shower curtain," the guard had ordered. One by one, we removed our shoes and did as she instructed.

I said a short prayer because I was afraid of how we would be searched. I knew the worst was yet to come. They need to be very careful that no one brings any kind of pills or substance, including cigarettes, into the prison.

I sought the LORD, and . . . he delivered me from all my fears.
—PSALM 34:4

I gave the female guard my license and she gave me a card with a number on it. It reminded me of when my husband and I had visited a minimum-security prison a few years before this. When the inmates' numbers were called, they had to line up like cattle called for slaughter just to be counted.

I remember thinking: *Thank God that when we all get to heaven, if these inmates have confessed Jesus as Savior and Lord, they will no longer be numbers, but their names will be written in the Lamb's book of life.*

Nothing impure will ever enter it, nor will anyone who does what is shameful or deceitful, but only those whose names are written in the Lamb's book of life.
—REVELATION 21:27

"Step inside the shower curtain," the guard yelled at me. I did as I was instructed. She pulled it around us while the other visitors waited outside. "Pull your pockets inside out," she directed.

Oh, great, I thought. My pockets wouldn't come all the way out. One was sewn in. I was nervous. I told her she could put her hand inside my pockets and check for drugs or whatever she was looking for. She didn't.

"Stick out your tongue!" she ordered. I did. "Lift it up . . . down . . . sideways . . . and shake out your shoes! Now, unsnap your bra and pull your shirt out of your pants."

Oh, no, I thought. *Here it comes!* The guard came over and went all up and down my body. Then she checked my hair to see if anything was hidden there, just like I used to check my boys' hair when someone at school had lice. I wanted to say something. I wanted her to know I was not a threat to their prison system.

As she searched me, I mentioned that my husband and I had been in prison ministry for several years and that I was bringing hope to an inmate. She listened.

Post Script

Shortly after this experience, I led Debbie to personal faith in Christ. I thanked God she had listened to God's call. Her brother knew the inmate I was visiting and began attending Bible study with him. I thanked God that he was also listening to God's call.

EVIL
EXPOSED

"Not by might, nor by power, but by my Spirit," says the LORD Almighty.
—ZECHARIAH 4:6

God's timing is never by chance!

You, Too?

Over the years, my family often went to the church camp where the youth pastor had molested me all those years ago. In the summer of 1998, I saw a childhood friend at the campground who had not been back in many years. We briefly spoke prior to an evening service and she asked what God was doing in my life. I told her He was pulling me into ministry with drug addicts, ex-cons and alcoholics on the streets. I had been called to the underdog! She told me that she too was working with addicts as a counselor in a rehabilitation center.

Even though there was no song or altar call at the end of that evening's service, I felt a poke on my arm. It was my friend. She wanted me to pray with her, so we went forward to the altar. I was in ministry with many hurting people but had no idea why she chose me to pray with her. I silently prayed: *God, You understand this dear sister's wounds because You suffered and died for each one of us and have taken our scars upon Your body on the cross. Would You now take her pain and allow me to pray with my childhood friend with compassion, as You would have me pray.*

Her words tumbled out—years of pain, defeat, sadness, emptiness, lone-liness, sorrow, addictions. When she included sexual abuse in the list, I put my hand over her mouth and said the name of the long-ago youth pastor. *Yes*, she nodded.

We began crying like babies when I told her, "He did it to me, too!" We wept and prayed together for our lost childhood, and I realized at once that God had brought us both back "home," full-circle so we could begin to deal with this.

Committee Formed

In November, my friend wrote to ask if I would be willing to come for-ward and help expose this man's sin. In her letter, she reminded me that "this addiction will not stop; it continues over and over with hundreds of victims. Statistics have shown that for every person violated by a molester, you can almost multiply that number by eight to see the extent of the prob-lem. If we were to do nothing, we would be allowing this sin to continue."

She had told her pastor's wife about the abuse, and the pastor's wife asked if there were any more victims my friend knew about. The pastor's wife then contacted the head of my childhood denomination with which the camp and the youth pastor were affiliated. Of course, by then the statute of limitations had run out as far as filing criminal charges. But since the campground and the former youth pastor were part of the denomination, the denominational leaders assembled a committee that spent many hours working diligently to uncover everything possible.

The Christian and Missionary Alliance had dealt with a highly publi-cized case just the year before that involved long-ago abuse at a school in Africa for missionary kids. They had worked very diligently to bring the truth to light and developed a protocol for dealing with future abuse issue and allegations.

We had the full support of the denomination. The committee sent out over twenty letters to childhood friends my friend and I identified as pos-sible victims of abuse or those we thought might have some knowledge of the abuse or know of others who had been molested. In the end, four of us women were willing to face this man at a hearing set for the next July.

The former youth pastor was interviewed for hours by a panel, includ-ing a well-known psychologist, but claimed no memory of the things of which he was accused. The denomination had brought six charges against him.

Post Script

The Christian and Missionary Alliance has also developed a child abuse prevention policy in a booklet entitled "Safe Place" that helps churches prevent this from happening to children in their churches! I am glad that the C&MA has determined to be proactive in regard to abuse issues in the church. Plus they are very responsive to abuse allegations, as you will see in this book.

I recently talked with a pastor in the denomination charged with overseeing the spiritual growth of pastors. Instead of ministry to further the kingdom of God, he sadly must devote a lot of his time to counseling. He told me that much of his time is spent in discipline and restoration ministry because of addictive behaviors.

THE
FLEECE

As I was reading my Bible one late spring day in 1999, I was asking God, "Am I really supposed to go forward with this?" I decided to ask Him for a sign just as Gideon had done in Judges 6:17: "If now I have found favor in your eyes, give me a sign that it is really you talking to me." In verses 36–40 of that chapter Gideon also put out a fleece and asked God to show him in an extraordinary way that God was going to use him to save Israel.

A Sign

The very next day as I watered my rosebush in front of our house, I could hardly believe what I saw! On one stem there were five roses. To me this represented the four women who would be facing this man, and Jesus was in the middle of us!

A Poem

My photographer husband took a picture of those roses. I wrote the following poem and just before the "trial" in July, I gave each woman a copy as I handed her a long-stemmed pink rose to hold while she gave her "testimony":

Your life is just like this rose:
fragile . . . beautiful . . . graceful . . .
fragrant with the beauty of Christ!
The thorns represent the painful circumstances
that we all have faced in life and the courage
it took to get us where we are.
They also represent the price Jesus paid on the cross for
your sins and His tremendous love for you!

INTENSE SPIRITUAL WARFARE

Journal Entries in June 1999

Satan is trying to defeat me from every possible angle prior to needing the courage to face this man! I am severely ill and experiencing weight loss, nausea, migraines, high temperatures, severe stomach cramps and no relief! The "trial" is only two weeks away!

The doctor prescribed a high-powered drug three times daily to treat me for a possible recurrence of the giardiasis I contracted two years ago in Tijuana, Mexico. (Giardia is a parasite you can get from food that is not washed carefully. If the larvae aren't completely killed, the illness can come back under stress)

I am VIOLENTLY ILL! Oh God, please help me! I can't eat. I have memory loss and scattered thinking. The drugs are making me sick! I called today for the elders of my church to anoint me and pray for me. I want to go off the drugs and trust God to heal me.

> Is any one of you sick? He should call the elders of the church to pray over him and anoint him with oil in the name of the Lord.
> —James 5:14

I needed the prayer of my church and I needed to tell the elders what I am facing. As they read what I had prepared for the "trial," one elder became angry and another wept!

Two days later: *Praise God! I felt a release in my body and my spirit today! I went to prayer meeting tonight and publicly gave praise for God's miraculous healing!*

One day after that: *I got a call from the doctor who tested me for Giardia. All tests are negative! I claim healing of mind, body and spirit!*

> He sent forth his word and healed them; he rescued them from the grave.
> —PSALM 107:20

Concerns

My daddy has always been there for me spiritually. But he was very concerned about my going forward with the plans to face this youth pastor. He knew this man.

He wept as I read him the words God had helped me very carefully prepare to read at the disciplinary committee hearing. I am sure he felt helpless to be able to walk through this with his daughter, so he encouraged me with the following scripture:

> Find rest, O my soul, in God alone; my hope comes from him. He alone is my rock and my salvation; he is my fortress, I will not be shaken. My salvation and my honor depend on God; he is my mighty rock, my refuge. Trust in him at all times, O people; pour out your hearts to him, for God is our refuge.
> —PSALM 62:5–8

He added, "When you face that man, you will be looking at Satan himself!"

"No, Daddy," I said. "Someone had to have hurt him so bad that he went on to hurt me so bad!" It's a hurt and wounded dog that goes on to bite another wounded dog.

Journal Entry—July 10, 1999

I am back at the camp where I was molested. I can't believe that in just one week I will face him!

I also can't believe how sick I am—again! Both my husband and I are being physically attacked with various forms of sickness. We were even sent by the camp nurse to an urgent care clinic.

101

God, when will this end? Take it away from us! I need to be whole!

We were treated by a warm and compassionate female doctor who empathized not only with our pain, but with my heartache as well. I wept when she knelt at my feet and said, "I have a friend who was molested." (Is she really talking about herself? I wondered) "When you write a book, would you please give me a copy?"

Writing about it is furthest thing from my mind!

Journal Entry—July 13, 1999

"Trial" is in three days . . . preparing . . . nervous!

The Next Day

One of my friends asked me to go with her back to the place at the campground where she had been molested. She hadn't faced her "demons" yet. She wanted to go with me to pray deliverance over that room. We got permission from the director who assured us, "no one is in that room . . . the place is empty."

Walking up the stairs, she commented, "I can't believe I let him take me here with bribes of comic books and candy!"

I reminded her that she was little and that it was not her fault. "He was the one who crossed those boundaries," I added. "You did not! He knew exactly what he was doing. Don't even go there."

As we walked down the long hallway I noticed that every door was open, except the door to the room she indicated was where she had been molested. We looked at one another and said nothing. She took a deep breath and knocked on the door.

A dark-haired man opened it, completely taking us off guard. We were shocked. He was tall and thin and had on a white shirt. He *looked* evil. And we both knew he didn't belong there in that room. (These are things I don't like to think of now, but people who have dealt with evil and demons will understand what we both experienced)

We ran! Both of us were shaking.

We went downstairs quickly and entered a room directly under that room. We had our Bibles with us and I asked her if she believed in spiritual warfare.

"No."

I simply told her, "If you spend any amount of time with me, you will!"

We prayed together, shared scripture the Lord had given us both, and prayed cleansing over the whole place!

Later when we told the camp director what had happened, he and others could not understand who was in that room!

My daddy was right. It was as if I had looked into the face of Satan himself!

> How can anyone enter a strong man's house and carry off his possessions unless he first ties up the strong man?
>
> —MATTHEW 12:29

Satan will not let anything go if he thinks he can keep it binding you!

We must renounce (let go of and be free from) things from our past—things that we've held on to or places we keep going back to. These are things we must get out of our house (out of our lives)—anything not of God—in order to let God in!

> Submit yourselves, then, to God. Resist the devil, and he will flee from you.
>
> —JAMES 4:7

Our faith must be active. Prayer, confession of sin, reading God's Word daily, fellowship with other believers and following His voice are all a part of the Christian faith.

Journal Entry—July 15, 1999

Relaxed on the beach with a friend.

July 16

The day before the "trial" and the day of our flight to Florida to face the accused. Two of us were going together. Our reservations had been made over a month ago and we had our tickets in hand. My parents met us at the airport. When we approached the counter, the ticket agent announced, "Your flight is canceled!"

My friend looked at me in disbelief.

"You've got to get us on another plane immediately," I said. "We face a 'trial' tomorrow and must get there as soon as possible!"

My friend nudged me and said, "I'm beginning to understand what you meant before!"

We booked another flight. My parents prayed over us. My friend and I comforted one another during that two-hour trip.

The airplane circled and circled the airport instead of landing. *Something was wrong!*

The flight attendant came on the speaker: "Because of a torrential rainstorm, the airport is closed."

We just looked at each other and prayed silently. *Satan, get out of our lives! We command you, in the name of Jesus to leave us alone!* We continued to pray that the plane wouldn't run out of gas.

The airport opened one-half hour later. My head was spinning from the flight. *Oh, God, please, please prepare me for what I have to do tomorrow!*

FACING THE ACCUSED

He reached down from on high and took hold of me; he drew me out of deep waters. He rescued me from my powerful enemy, from my foes, who were too strong for me. They confronted me in the day of my disaster, but the LORD was my support. He brought me out into a spacious place; he rescued me because he delighted in me.

—PSALM 18:16–19

July 17, 1999—Florida

Running on adrenaline. Only two hours of sleep. Panic! Can I do this? Questions.

I called my husband at 4:30 A.M. No answer. Went over all my notes, prayed, worried. I am scared to death! I can't wait until this is all over! They told me I could call anyone, so I called my parents and a friend. They prayed with me.

The four of us who were going to testify were given the VIP treatment by the denomination. We stayed in a beautiful hotel and were given spending money for our meals and other needs. Two of the committee members' wives (pastors' wives) were available to lend a listening ear and support us emotionally. A Christian psychologist was also available to us.

The committee heard each of us individually. Each of us was ushered into the room where the hearing took place one at a time, spoke to the committee and then was escorted out of the room before the next woman was brought in.

When the committee chairman, a pastor, came and got me, I honestly don't know how I got up to the top floor of the hotel where the hearing took place.

What does he look like after forty-four years? I told myself he is old. What an experience! *What if my mind goes blank like it did when I had piano recitals or took a test at school?* Sexual abuse victims have problems with remembering because in order to survive they've had to blank out huge chunks of their memories. I had to remind myself to take deep breaths. My hands were ice cold!

> Even though I walk through the valley of the shadow of death, I will fear
> no evil, for you are with me.
>
> —Psalm 23:4

OK, I can do this. God, You are with me and these pastors are with me, too. I knew that all of these men knew the accused and had been most generous in their support of me and the other women.

The eight pastors on the committee sat around the conference table. They had told me "he" would be sitting next to the psychologist who was sitting next to me, so I couldn't see him directly. A tape recorder and a microphone were on the table in front of me.

The format of the hearing was outlined: We would start with prayer and then I could speak as long as necessary. The accused would then be given an opportunity to speak to me if he wanted to. (*Oh boy, did I need prayer!*) But the accused probably needed it more than I did.

I felt so unprepared as I began my testimony. I had been preparing for this for months, but something was wrong! *Why were they rewinding the tape?* They asked me to speak louder. Then it struck me that they were older and having a hard time hearing my timid voice.

I also realized that I had not scraped together enough courage to look at "him." *Courage, Barb, courage.* I turned sideways to face the youth pastor who was no longer young as I remembered him. He looked weak. My heart went out to him. My voice suddenly was strong. I felt more at ease. *Oh, God, I wasn't prepared for this!*

He smiled at me. I certainly didn't expect that! I was sad and felt pity for him. His appearance was unkempt. He was disheveled and was wearing an untucked white shirt (much like the man in the "unoccupied" room at the campground!) and his yellow teeth looked as if they were glued together. I saw an addict sitting at that table—not unlike those to whom I had been called to minister.

He was all alone. I was not!

My
Testimony

I reached past the psychologist and handed "him" a picture of an eleven-year-old girl, standing tall and skinny and with a very sad face. I also gave a copy of the photo to each of the pastors. The child in the picture was me. I told "him," "Here is a picture of the little girl you molested. I know you don't know who I am now, but you will remember this child. The adult woman before you now is courageous and strong, but I wanted you to remember this child as I speak to you."

Then I asked him a question. "Do know what your name means? And has anyone ever given you a scripture card with your name on it?"

"No."

I had bought scripture name cards many times, giving them to those to whom we ministered who had served prison time. I would remind them that in prison they were just a number, but if they accepted Jesus as Savior and Lord, their names would be written in the Lamb's Book of Life. (See Revelation 21:27)

I told him, "Your name means 'kingly.'" He looked at me with a startled expression. "But," I continued, "you haven't lived up to your name."

Addressing the Accused

I then read my prepared testimony, addressing my remarks to him—but not really looking at him—for almost an hour. I told him exactly what I remember him doing to me as he molested me and how I remember exactly what I had on and what he looked like. One of the other things I said to him was: "Somehow, I am not angry at you, but at the sin against me." God led me. I felt His presence. After I was finished, I turned to him and said I had one last question to ask, but that I didn't want him to answer right away.

I asked him to sit there and think about it for a couple of minutes because I wanted to hear his answer clearly. "Who hurt you so bad that you had to hurt me so bad?" I asked. I knew the Holy Spirit was speaking through me because this was definitely not something I had intended to ask him.

His answer was: "I, like you, was saved at a very early age. I don't recall being sexually molested." He thanked me for coming and then he said something the committee and I never thought we would hear: "Can you ever find it in your heart to forgive me?" Was this an admission of guilt? The committee chairman had told me he had been in complete denial up to this point. I looked at him and told him that from what I knew about the pattern of a molester, he had probably hurt hundreds of innocent little children.

Then I said, "I don't know if you asked for my forgiveness because you got caught, or if it is sincerely from your heart. But I never could have come here to face you if I hadn't already forgiven you. Yes, you have my forgiveness!"

Continuing, I asked him if he had ever been to an Alcoholics Anonymous meeting.

He surprised me by saying, "Yes."

I took out my New International Version Recovery Devotional Bible, which we had been given by one of the ex-cons we were mentoring. It is the most wonderful, helpful, healing Bible I have ever seen. Designed especially for those who are recovering from addictive, compulsive or codependent behavior patterns, this Bible encourages a person to improve his or her relationship with God through focused prayer and meditation.

In addition to the full text of the New International Version of the Bible, there is a year's worth of daily meditations that include insights selected from the writings of several experts in the recovery field. Other helps include introductions for each book of the Bible that highlight its recovery-related themes, as well as a variety of reading plans. Another feature is the "Step markers" that relate scriptures to the steps in twelve-step programs like Alcoholics Anonymous, Adult Children of Alcoholics, Codependents Anonymous, as well as programs that deal with sexual (and other) addictions.

I told him that sin has consequences and began reading the twelve steps to him. (I don't know if the pastors in the room had ever heard them before)

I stopped at Step 4: "Take a searching and moral inventory of yourself."

Then I read Step 5: "Admit to God, to ourselves, and to another human being the exact nature of our wrongs."

I stopped after I read Step 9: "Make amends to those people you have harmed," and said to him, "It isn't possible for you to do that. Too much time has gone by.

I ended by saying, "You need to run into recovery just as I have done! You have these wonderful men of God here to help you begin to deal with all the damage that was done to you!" I never put him in a box any differently than I was in during my recovery.

> I will keep you and will make you to be a covenant for the people, to restore the land and to reassign its desolate inheritances, to say to the captives, "Come out," and to those in darkness, "Be free!"
> —ISAIAH 49:8–9

Post Script

This man was found guilty on all six counts the committee had brought against him, five of which pertained to the abuse. One of those involved the severe emotional and psychological damage done as a result of the molestation of the four women who were willing to face him. The sixth count was for allegedly withholding information from the disciplinary committee.

He was expelled from any further ministry including any and all contact with children, specifically in the church. His ministerial license was revoked.

After the "trial," he never admitted to anything ever again.

Seven weeks later, he died after falling and breaking his back. He died a disheveled and broken man!

> As heat and drought snatch away the melted snow, so the grave snatches away those who have sinned. The womb forgets them, the worm feasts on them; evil men are no longer remembered but are broken like a tree.
> —JOB 24:19–20

MEETING KURT

L ater that day, it finally hit me that it was all over! I felt so relieved in my spirit. I experienced an instant release and decided to relax by the beautiful outdoor spa and pool at the hotel since I wasn't leaving until noon the next day for my flight home to Boston. God had begun to open me up to so many people already.

Poolside Chat

I wasn't looking for anyone in particular to talk to when I saw a young man who appeared to be in his late thirties sitting at the edge of the pool. I put my feet in the cool water and said, "Hi, my name's Barb." The thing that struck me first was the cross around his neck. He also had a ponytail and lots of tattoos and reminded me of the many motorcyclists we ministered to. So I asked him if he was with anyone and if he wanted to talk.

As he moved closer, he said his name was Kurt and that he was alone. (I hoped he didn't think that I was coming on to him) I then saw the cross earring in his ear and asked if the cross he was wearing had any significance to him. He told me he was not religious but I could tell in my spirit that he desired to know God. He asked me if I was a Christian.

"Yes," I told him, and asked him why he was at the hotel.

"I'm a bodybuilder and am interested in opening a business in the area. Why are you here?"

I told him that I had just gotten the courage to bring a pastor into the light who had molested me years ago and that it was one of the hardest things I had ever done in my life!

Kurt shook his head in disbelief.

"How can I pray for you?" I asked.

He told me his forty-two-year-old brother had suffered a heart attack. "Would you pray for him?" he asked me. "He has two kids and a wife." He sadly told me that his mother had died a year ago from a stroke and how badly he felt that he wasn't able to be there to hold her hand when she died.

My heart went out to this deeply wounded man.

As we easily chatted, I told him that everyone has a God-shaped hole inside that only God could fill. "If we don't fill it up with Him," I told Kurt, "we will fill it up with other things."

He listened as I mentioned how Satan always tempts us in our minds before we act, and I asked him if I could go to my room and get a Four Spiritual Laws booklet that would explain the way of salvation to him. I added that I'd like him to have a cassette tape of my interview on the radio about reaching out to an alcoholic/heroin addict. It was also in my room. I told him that God had told me to put the tape in my suitcase so I could give it to someone. I told him he must be that "someone."

He seemed receptive to this and gave me his room number. He was going out with his buddies for dinner that evening and asked me to put the tape and booklet under his door. When I got back to my room, I called his room to suggest I meet him in the lobby instead. (I just felt it would look better)

I got to the lobby before Kurt did and saw one of the pastors who had served on the discipline and restoration committee. I was running out of Four Spiritual Laws booklets and asked him if he could get me more. I also told him about my conversation with Kurt and asked him to pray for Kurt.

The Next Day

I had the best night's sleep because I had nothing on my mind and realized I was free from my burdens. On Friday, I had two hours to relax poolside before taking the shuttle to the airport. My thinking was interrupted when I heard a male voice call my name. I was surprised to see Kurt pull up a chaise lounge.

"Mind if I join you?" he asked.

"No," I told him. "I've been praying for you."

He seemed like he wanted to unload. "I binged last night. My buddies and I partied and drank."

"You were right," he continued. "The devil whispered in my ear, 'Go ahead and have one—it won't hurt you.'" He told me that drinking had been the cause of his problems, and added that he was divorced, had no kids and lived with his dad.

"Can you add one more person to your prayer list?" he asked.

I laughed when I realized how easily I was able to share with a complete stranger who wanted to know more about God. "Sure, who is it?"

"Scooter, my cousin who is my best friend. He has a successful career, but he is obsessed with being a priest and wants to enter the seminary before he gets too old. He's forty years old but is struggling with having to be celibate."

He agreed with me when I told him that being celibate was unnatural for a man, but if Scooter was struggling with his decision, maybe God didn't want him to be a priest.

He thanked me for taking the time to talk with him and said he couldn't wait to show the booklet to Scooter and have him listen to the tape.

As he hugged me goodbye, I asked him to write to me when he made a decision for Christ.

"I won't write. I'll call you!" he promised.

Kurt, I'm still praying that you'll call.

PSALM 23

During the years I was sexually abused, I felt so alone. In coming out of the darkness, I felt as if no one fully understood the burden I was carrying.

The Holy Spirit began to minister to me as I read Psalm 23. I remembered hearing my preacher daddy read this psalm at funerals, so I related it to death. Although I wasn't dealing with physical death, I *was* dealing with a deep wound in my spirit, which was an emotional death.

As I struggled with feelings of abandonment, I wondered if God heard my cries of pain. I began to see myself as the Good Shepherd saw me, as He lovingly and gently started restoring my wounded soul back to life.

If God brings you to it, He will bring you through it.

—AUTHOR UNKNOWN

NIV Recovery Devotional Bible	**Inspired by God's Holy Spirit**

1. "The LORD is my shepherd, I shall not be in want."

1. My Recovery Bible says that "shall not be in want" means now, in our present circumstances. Our Shepherd wants us not to walk in bondage to our past, but in freedom, in spite of our circumstances.

2. "He makes me lie down in green pastures, he leads me besides quiet waters,"

2. "Green pastures" signify growth, life, springtime, grass, buds, flowers, warmth and beauty out of lifeless, cold winter and death.
Lord, help me not to run ahead of You. Make me quiet before you, listening to Your still, small voice as I sit by streams of living water to quench my parched dry spirit.

3. "he restores my soul.
He guides me in paths of righteousness
for his name's sake."

3. Deep wounds from my childhood are healed as I am brought into spiritual wholeness.
Like the blind being led by a guide dog, I want to hold on to the Good Shepherd who directs me with His staff of protection.
He steers me in the right direction. His way, not mine. His Spirit leading, not self or the flesh.
I am the daughter of the King of Kings!

4. "Even though I walk through the valley of the shadow of death, I will fear no evil, for you are with me;

4. Forest? Jungle? Briers? Thick trees? No way out? Can't see my way ahead? Circumstances of my life? Panic?
I must trust in God, not in myself. In spite of my fears, when I cannot see what lies ahead, I won't be afraid!
I am not alone!

your rod and your staff, they comfort me."

Like a little lost lamb, I am pulled back from the crooked, briery path of rocks that are hard to walk on.
My feet are steadied as the Shepherd walks along by my side to keep me from stumbling and scraping my knees.

5. "You prepare a table before me in the presence of my enemies.

5. A feast is wonderfully prepared for my starving soul,
even in the midst of those who doubt my abilities, or those who may have lied or distorted the truth as they tried to understand what God has birthed in this child.

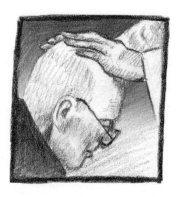

You anoint my head with oil;

With the love of the Father, Son and Holy Spirit, You put healing balm on my head, and God's anointing flows from me to others.

my cup overflows."

I am awed and so filled with thanksgiving and blessing at what the Father is doing that I can hardly contain it! I begin sharing and giving back what I have learned to those who are broken in spirit and wounded in soul.

6. "Surely goodness and love will follow me

6. No more harm, but good, will come to me. Heart-wrenching pain is replaced by God's mercy! "Blessed are the merciful for they will be shown mercy" (Matthew 5:7). This kind of love is extravagant! This love steps in when it is inconvenient! Mercy extends a hand to the person who has done you immeasurable harm, or caused you loss or pain. Mercy pleads for leniency. Mercy, love and goodness say, "Father, forgive them."

all the days of my life, and I will dwell in the house of the LORD forever."

My heavenly Father assures me of these promises. And a crown of righteousness and Heaven are mine for all eternity!

THE BLIND MAN RECEIVES HIS SIGHT

Some people brought a blind man and begged Jesus to touch him. He took the blind man by the hand and led him outside the village. When he had spit on the man's eyes and put his hands on him, Jesus asked, "Do you see anything?" He looked up and said, "I see people; they look like trees walking around." Once more Jesus put his hands on the man's eyes. Then his eyes were opened, his sight was restored, and he saw everything clearly.

—MARK 8:22–25

Being a Light in the Darkness

God has called me to do the work of an evangelist, to share the light of God's truth with everyone I meet. When I was a little girl in Sunday school, we used to sing one of my favorite songs, "This Little Light of Mine." Even before I could read, I knew all the words by heart. I belted them out: "This little light of mine, I'm gonna let it shine, let it shine, let it shine, let it shine."

I would wave my finger in the air as if it were a lit candle. I meant every word as I sang it because Jesus was in my heart and deep in my soul. When we worship God, we give our praise back to Him. On and on I'd sing: "Hide it under a bushel? No! I'm gonna let it shine, let it shine, let it shine." I would cover up my "candle" finger with my other hand and take my hand away and stomp my foot as I sang "No!"

Leo, the Hitchhiker

Leo was hitchhiking that summer day in 1999. It was something he did every day for the eighteen years he had been back in town. I never pick up hitchhikers, but it was different with Leo because I knew him from around town and had given him rides a couple of times before.

Everyone in Milford knew Leo. He grew up in our town and, other than a stint or two of living on the West Coast, lived in Milford for the majority of his life. Because he became blind in 1979, Leo always walked carefully and slowly with his white cane. Leo suffered a broken hip in May 1984 when a kid knocked him to the sidewalk. He ended up spending three months in the VA hospital to recuperate. He's been knocked over other times since, often by what he calls "punks." He told me that after the first time of being knocked over, he had learned how to fall!

Although his body had been bruised, he was strong in spirit. He had spunk, and I liked him when I read the account of his 1984 "mishap" in the newspaper.

Getting Better Acquainted

God had a purpose for Leo and me to get better acquainted that day in 1999. I have permission to tell part of his story.

As I drove past him, I thought about all of the errands I had to do that day. But I felt compassion for him as he sat on a stone wall. He wore his sunglasses and held his white cane with one hand, using his other thumb to hitchhike. It was a scorching hot day. My car had air-conditioning. I backed up, pushed the passenger door open and said, "Hop in."

He recognized my voice and called me by name. He asked me what was going on in my life since I had last given him a ride. I told him that I was about to face a man who had betrayed and victimized me years ago.

"You are unlike most people I have ever met," he said.

I told him I was a Christian.

He said, "You are a woman of conviction and courage. Christians are the most compassionate of all people!"

I told him that by God's grace I was able to do something this hard, knowing that it is in the hard places that God always has something for us to learn. Then I asked Leo a question that I had never asked anyone before. "Leo, have you ever had a personal encounter with Jesus Christ as your personal Savior and Lord? Because if you did, you would be able to tell me the exact time and date?"

His Story

"1977," he answered immediately. "It was a lady just like you who invited me to her church in California where I was living at the time. It was then that I invited Him into my heart. I heard such wonderful sermons at that church, and when I couldn't get there, she sent the messages on tapes to me.

"I met this woman in a VA surplus store while I was looking at blue jeans," he continued. "I was bawling my eyes out and didn't know why I was crying. She came over to me and asked what was wrong and if there was anything she could do to help me. She had the same kind of compassion that you have. I couldn't tell her why I was crying because I cried day and night for many months. (I found out later when I was medically diagnosed that it was a brain tumor that caused the crying spells) This woman invited me to join her for coffee and took me to a chapel where she listened to me. She promised to pray for me and invited me to her church."

I listened intently as he told me his painful story. "I am a World War II vet, brought up in an Irish-Catholic family. I was an altar boy for years and became blind in 1979 because of a brain tumor. At one time, I was the manager for a major jazz orchestra and knew many of the big-name jazz performers of that era. I love to review and critique jazz music, but because the part of my brain that controls my emotions was affected by the tumor, I can no longer write. I can write the words, but words without heart don't mean a thing."

As an author, I expressed sadness that he could no longer write, and I asked him to go on.

"God is personal to me," he continued, "but I don't go to church. My ears are too sensitive. The music is too loud. I worship God in my own way in my gardens and outdoors. I turned against the Catholic church years ago because it is filled with hypocrites!

"One time, I heard a homily at church about the Good Samaritan. Because I was blind, after the service, I asked four different people to give me a ride home. None responded. As I trudged home that day, a man who didn't know the Lord—but did know me—gave me a ride home. I never went back to that church again, but I still have my faith.

"When I became blind in 1979, the surgeon apologized. He had to remove a large tumor from my brain. That tumor was what had caused the unexplainable crying jags I had experienced and perhaps even the seizures I had experienced in 1946 shortly after I got out of the Navy. The surgeon said that my sight might come back in fifteen or twenty years because of something called 'aberrant regeneration.'

"I once owned a growing lumber business here in town, but when I became blind, I lost everything—even my dog!"

I felt so much empathy towards him.

"I had lapsed into a coma during the surgery when I had a stroke. The coma lasted for five weeks after the surgery," he continued. "When I finally came out of the coma, I became depressed and very angry! I had to work through all my emotions, including being estranged from my family." He finished by saying, "I may not be able to write, but I can still sing!"

I encouraged him to continue to praise the Lord even in the midst of his difficulties. He has told me since what a great comfort Psalm 38 has been to him over the years.

When we arrived at his destination that day in 1999, I felt like I had just spent time with God. I asked Leo how I could pray for him before he got out of my car.

Not really answering my question, he took both of my hands in his and kissed them. "You see the sign outside that store?" he asked. Answering his own question, he said, "It says 'Honey Dew Donuts.'"

"Leo, you can see?"

"Yes, God gave me back my sight!"

I was practically crying and asked him if I could pray with him. As we bowed our heads, I praised God for giving him back his sight. Then, before we parted, he again took my hands in his and kissed them.

No one lights a lamp and puts it in a place where it will be hidden, or under a bowl. Instead he puts it on its stand, so that those who come in may see the light. Your eye is the lamp of your body. When your eyes are good, your whole body also is full of light. But when they are bad, your body also is full of darkness. See to it, then, that the light within you is not darkness. Therefore, if your whole body is full of light, and no part of it dark, it will be completely lighted, as when the light of a lamp shines on you.

—LUKE 11:33–35

There is no lovelier way to thank God for your sight than by giving a helping hand to someone in the dark.

—HELEN KELLER

GIGGLES DAY

There is a time for everything, and a season for every activity under heaven: a time to be born and a time to die, . . . a time to kill and a time to heal, a time to tear down and a time to build, a time to weep and a time to laugh, a time to mourn and a time to dance.

—ECCLESIASTES 3:1–4

Friday, September 21, 2000

Julie, the most precious of all jewels and God's gift to me, made an appointment with me today so we could have what she called a "Giggles Day." She told me, "One of the things I love about you, Barb, is your spontaneous laugh!" I told her that my middle name is Joy, a name a couple of my friends call me.

Julie came over and we shared what Christ was doing in our lives with one another. Because she was just a new Christian, she was struggling. She wanted a deeper walk with God and took a day off from her job because as she put it, "stuff is crowding Jesus out!"

Julie wanted to know about my personal walk with God. She had many questions. "Has your life always been this deep?" she asked me. "Share your journey of faith with me, Barb."

I began to do that while she took me on a surprise shopping adventure! I had no idea where we were going, but I loved the openness of her spirit and genuineness of her faith in me as her friend. We chatted and giggled like little children running through the sprinkler on a hot summer day! I hadn't felt this good in a long, long time!

She took me to a shop called "Bibles, Books and Things" right here in Milford. There, she gave me the greatest gift she could ever give me: a gift certificate so I could shower the people God is bringing into my life with love!

Julie owns her own business and became a Christian at our church in the New Beginnings Class. She had befriended an ex-con, an ex-heroin addict, and when he graduated from a drug treatment program, I had helped her organize a graduation party for him. Another time she wrote a check to help a young single mom I was mentoring who was struggling to pay her rent. This was such a special blessing to those people. And Julie was such a blessing to me!

"You can buy anything you think they need," she told me. "A Recovery Devotional Bible, Christian books, or maybe a CD." Then she picked out a gospel rap CD for my friend's fourteen-year-old daughter and a couple of recovery books for the single mom I was mentoring. She bought a book for someone we had been reaching out to and mentoring for several years who was back in prison.

Finally, she picked out a big coffee mug for a new Christian, an ex-con I had led to the Lord. It had an eagle on it and this verse: "But those who hope in the LORD will renew their strength. They will soar on wings like eagles; they will run and not grow weary, they will walk and not be faint" (Isaiah 40:31). I thought to myself, *Oh, Lord, please help him to soar above his problems!*

On our way home Julie said, "Barb, now I know how it feels to give back! I've been too centered on myself, my job and my family. Thank you for teaching me!"

No, Julie, thank you, for being obedient to His call!

Barbara Joy

Several years ago, my father bought me a special gift, a mug with my name on it. I enjoy learning about what names mean. One of the meanings of my name is *beautiful stranger*. According to the inscription on the mug, it also means *mystery* with the following explanation: "You are mysterious, secretive, and employ subtle methods to achieve your goals. You have an inner self that only those closest to you will ever know."

MIRACULOUS HEALINGS

He sent forth his word and healed them; he rescued them from the grave.
—PSALM 107:20

During the times of the intense ministry God has called me to I have noticed a distinct pattern in relation to my physical health. I have always enjoyed good health, but with this calling, Satan knows just where he can get his foot in the door in an effort to defeat what God has started. When you least expect it, he will try to get in any way he can!

While I was ministering to what Jesus calls, "the least of these," my body was under attack. I developed several physical problems within just a short time. Three doctors told me that I had bone loss, degeneration of my kneecaps, osteoporosis, and a chronic yeast infection. One problem would have been devastating in itself, but several were unbelievable! I refused to give into the enemy's attacks, because I knew that's where they were coming from and that God could heal me if He chose to do so.

For instance, during the eight months of 2001 that I suffered from the chronic yeast infection, I was deep into ministering to a Jewish woman who desperately needed to find Y'shua, her Messiah. She was a biker who was plagued with demons. She had been brutally wounded in her childhood and came across my e-mail address when she heard one of the miracle stories I had written and sent to another biker.

Medical and Spiritual Intervention

I believe completely in going to doctors, but I also believe that we should go to God with all our problems, including physical ones. I took prescription medication for the osteoporosis and the yeast infection and began doing prescribed exercises for both the bone loss and the knee problems.

I also began to fast and pray, and we asked our Christian Motorcyclists Association chapter president to anoint both my husband and myself with oil. He and other friends also prayed over us and used scripture verses to pray against the powers of darkness. God also used Christian music to minister deeply to my spirit. The more Christian music I played, the stronger I began to feel. I refused to give in to the enemy and his evil schemes after I had come so far.

Putting on the Armor

The Bible says that, as believers, we should put on the full armor of God to be able to withstand the fiery darts of the devil. I opened my Bible and this is what I read:

> Finally, be strong in the Lord and in his mighty power. Put on the full armor of God so that you can take your stand against the devil's schemes. For our struggle is not against flesh and blood, but against the rulers, against the authorities, against the powers of this dark world and against the spiritual forces of evil.
>
> —EPHESIANS 6:10–12

The more I read, the more I understood. God wants us to put on this full armor of God by immersing ourselves in His Word "so that when the day of evil comes, you may be able to stand your ground" (Ephesians 6:13).

God says that we are to have "the belt of truth [His Word] buckled around our waist" (Ephesians 6:14). If we want to receive His power, we need to read His Word, which is His love letter to us. I remembered back to the day when God spoke to me after the conference when my spiritual life was dry. I never wanted to be that dry ever again!

Ephesians 6:14 also instructs us to "stand firm." I see that as God desiring honesty and firmness in my life. But as a victim of abuse who had been living for decades in denial, my life sure had not been honest.

I was coming clean! It felt good. Jesus was healing my mind!

As I continued to read, I saw that God wants my "feet fitted with the readiness that comes from the gospel of peace" (Ephesians 6:15). God certainly wants us to share the gospel with others and live at peace with one another.

"In addition to this, take up the shield of faith, with which you can extinguish all the flaming arrows of the evil one" (Ephesians 6:16). So, my faith needs to be constantly strong in order to kick the devil back to hell where he belongs!

I continued reading: "Take the helmet of salvation and the sword of the Spirit, which is the word of God" (Ephesians 6:17). It was stated so clearly in scripture. I would begin to use God's Word in this battle against these physical attacks and not be defeated in my mind.

Healings

God personally gave me verses to claim for each of my healings. He also sent deliverance!

> He sent forth his word and healed them; he rescued them from the grave.
> —PSALM 107:20

God healed me completely of osteoporosis. After initially diagnosing me and prescribing medication, the doctor ordered another bone scan eighteen months later. He was amazed when that scan showed that I had absolutely no bone loss—not even what he had seen before. I knew it was an answer to prayer. In August of 2000, I was taken completely off the medications for osteoporosis.

> In you my soul takes refuge. I will take refuge in the shadow of your wings until the disaster [I wrote "violent storm" in my Bible] has passed.
> —PSALM 57:1

In November of 2001, my eight-month ordeal with chronic yeast infections was over and I was taken off that medication.

> The LORD brings death and makes alive; he brings down to the grave and raises up.
> —1 SAMUEL 2:6

In December of 2001, I wrote in my Bible that God had healed me of my knee problems when after a year of treatments, the orthopedic doctor said I didn't need to come back unless I had problems. I haven't had any problems since then. And I don't expect to be in his office any time soon!

God knew that I did not have time to waste with physical limitations while doing His work for His kingdom. I claim His complete healing in all of these areas.

For the word of God is living and active.

—HEBREWS 4:12

GOD'S DESIGNER ORIGINAL

O LORD, you are our Father. We are the clay, you are the potter; we are the work of your hand.

—ISAIAH 64:8

O ur son Jon always knew he would become an artist. He drew on everything, including his test papers, much to the amusement of some of his teachers. When he was a student at the Art Institute of Boston, he was introduced to the potter's wheel.

The Work of the Potter

The potter begins his work of art with a simple, nondescript lump of clay. The process of shaping the finished product is very slow. Water is used to keep the clay from sticking to the potter's hands. The work is not particularly even, and great care must be taken. Grit, pebbles and dirt must be removed from the clay. This time-consuming process must happen before the potter perfects the work and the piece is ready for the kiln.

The firing in the kiln takes place at incredibly hot temperatures. And it often takes several times in the kiln for the piece of art to meet the standards of the artist in order to become a beautifully finished piece of art.

God, the Potter

In Psalm 139, King David wrote a song to the Lord that is pretty much summed up in verse 14: "I praise you because I am . . . wonderfully made."

Each of us has been uniquely created by the Master Potter. And, from the very beginning, He has a plan for what He wants each of us to become. We are not mass-produced. Just like snowflakes, there are no two of us alike. Everything about each one of us is unique. If we yield our will to the Potter, we allow Him to take the grit and dirt away from our minds and hearts. He also wants to wash away our sins with the cleansing of His blood through His work on the cross. The firing is necessary to prepare us to do His work on this earth. Sometimes there must be several firings in order for us to become the beautiful designer originals He has created us to be.

He can use our eyes, our hands, our ears and our feet to fulfill His purpose on earth *if* we yield to His call to do it His way. Then our heart will beat with His in the image of Christ!

God has done that kind of work in my life. I started as a simple lump of clay in His hands, something not very pretty. I had to be cleansed by the washing of His blood shed on the cross for me, and lots of impurities had to be removed from my life. That had to be the work of God in my life. And those trips through the fire were almost unbearable. They hurt, but that's what it took for God to shape me into the work of art He had in mind from eternity past. But I'm still a work in progress!

> "O house of Israel, can I not do with you as this potter does?" declares the Lord. "Like clay in the hand of the potter, so are you in my hand."
> —JEREMIAH 18:6

Post Script

Patsy Clairmont uses this same pottery image in her book, *God Uses Cracked Pots*. Although her book is a lighthearted look at life's foibles and fears, her main premise is that it is only through our imperfections—the cracks, if you will—that God's light shines out of us to others. The imperfections, the hurts, in my life—or your life—are God's way of modeling healing to others. With His light inside, we can shine for His glory, even—and especially—in the broken places of our lives.

A Motorcycle, Prayers and a Miracle

O n April 10, 2001, I was on my way home from my part-time job late in the afternoon. Out of the corner of my eye I saw a guy ride past me on a motorcycle. Because my husband and I are members of the Christian Motorcyclists Association, I took more than a glance when I saw that he was riding an antique army green World War II Harley-Davidson motorcycle that had its original saddle bags. I remember wishing I could be out riding on that beautiful sunny afternoon. And riding that bike would be a nice touch!

Just seconds later, I saw a police car come alongside my car and then pass me.

In horror, I saw the biker ahead of me. He was sprawled on the sidewalk in front of Dunkin' Donuts, and the twisted metal of his Harley was crumpled on the sidewalk. My heart was pounding! I waited for the police to direct traffic around the scene and pulled into Dunkin' Donuts. Bikers take care of their own. Here was one of my biker brothers, and he was critically wounded.

How Could I Help?

I watched helplessly as the medics and fire personnel cared for him. A friend of mine who saw the accident said that he had flown over his handlebars like a rag doll, doing a triple somersault fifty-four feet into the air! His helmet was split in half and the medics were cutting off his clothes.

The elderly gentleman who hit him had been temporarily blinded by the sun and was talking with the police officers. My heart went out to him, too, as I watched him helplessly walking on the side of the road while he picked up the pieces of license plate and plastic bumper. *He must feel awful,* I thought.

I knew I had to do something and silently began praying, *God, have compassion on this man! Don't let him die! Save his soul!*

Other bystanders were in shock. There was blood on the sidewalk where he had landed, and we all could see the huge lump on his temple. My heart pounded as I waited for the ambulance to leave. I handed my Christian Motorcyclists Association card with my name and address on it to one of the police officers. I told him that I was a Christian from CMA and asked if I could have the injured man's name and phone number with the promise that our chapter would lift him up to God in prayer. He obliged, giving me the information I was seeking. I thanked him and left.

When I got home, the whole experience hit me like a ton of bricks! I noticed I was shaking. I got on my computer and e-mailed off an urgent request asking others to join me in prayer. I asked God for a miracle of healing for this man.

I tried to get in touch with someone from his family, but no one was home. I left a message on their answering machine to let them know I and others were praying for the injured man. Two days later, I got a phone call from his mother. She was crying as she thanked me for praying for her eldest son.

She said she had told him he shouldn't even be alive with the injuries he sustained. She told me that because of our prayers, the protrusion on his temple was totally gone the very next day and that he was already home from the hospital. He had a slight fracture in his leg and a concussion, but God had indeed answered my prayers and spared his life.

Three days later, a couple of our CMA friends, my husband and I rode our motorcycles over to meet him face-to-face. I could hardly believe that this was the same man that I had seen sprawled on the sidewalk and that he was sitting alive in front of me.

The prayer of a righteous man is powerful and effective.

—James 5:16

Post Script

My husband and I have stayed in touch with the older gentleman who hit the biker. We've had him and his lady friend over for dinner several times. They also join us occasionally at church for worship services and dinner theater productions. On an evening when I had another meeting, a friend of mine from church led her to faith in Christ. "She was so ready that evening during prayer meeting," my friend related. In her childlike innocence she asked my friend to pray that she would be happy.

My friend eagerly shared the plan of salvation with her and she said, "Oh, that would be nice" and prayed to ask Jesus into her life.

The gentleman had walked away from his Jewish faith. We were able to help him reconnect with his Jewish roots by inviting him to a Messianic Jewish congregation. People in Messianic Jewish congregations understand one another and the traditions from their Jewish roots, and worship Y'shua, the true Messiah.

SIGGI

Siggi called my house because of the letter to the editor I had written to our local newspaper about the motorcycle accident. He explained that his real name is Siegfried, but that I could call him "Siggi," like Ziggy, the cartoon character. I liked him immediately.

In his heavy German accent, he told me he used to be a biker and was familiar with the Christian Motorcyclists Association that I had mentioned in the letter to the editor. I liked him even more! Then, as soon as he told me he was a writer of songs and a Christian, I knew we had a lot in common. He explained that he writes day and night much like I do.

He said he had felt inspired to write a song about the ministry of CMA. I was delighted when I finally got to hear it, and I was soon playing it for all my CMA friends. It has a catchy little tune and you can hear the roar of motorcycles in the background.

Getting Better Acquainted

Siggi and his wife, Zita, soon invited us over so we could finally meet. We rode there on my husband's Honda Shadow Ace Tourer motorcycle. We immediately bonded as we began to share the painful stories of our lives.

They told us how the French Moroccan troops moved into their little town in Germany and took over the churches and arrested the preachers. Many churches were bombed, homes were attacked, and churches were burned.

136

When Zita was a child, the soldiers held a gun to her mother's head as she held her young grandson in her arms. The baby's mother, Zita's sister-in-law, hurried Zita and her cousin to the attic to hide and hopefully escape.

The pain was raw and the tears were still close to the surface. She spoke of the lights being shot out while the soldiers did anything they wanted, which included raping the neighborhood women and killing innocent victims.

She and Siggi both remember seeing and hearing that the belt buckles of both the Germans and Hitler had "God with us" inscribed on them.

Their eyes told the stories of those painful memories imbedded deeply in their hearts and minds. I was touched by their stories of betrayal and persecution. Although unlike my own story, the pain was the same. It didn't take long before we became good friends.

One day I asked Siggi if he would pray about something. I had seen his large recording studio in their home. Knowing how gifted he was, I asked him to write my song. A few days later he invited us over to their house and I tearfully listened to Siggi's song written for me.

Victorious Survivor

Words and music by Siegfried John Loh

This is no rap! This is a slap in the perpetrator's face!
I'm the victim no longer,
But a VICTORIOUS SURVIVOR!
I came out better, stronger.
I'm a victim no more!
There's a light inside me
That'll shine and guide me
Through God's healing power
To be happy once more!
(*Spoken*) *Oh, yes, I'm tellin' ya: I'm a Victorious Survivor!*
There's a new revival in the air.
Open up . . . confession everywhere!
Comin' out of darkness, feelin' free!
I was blind, but now I can see!
I've been lied at, spied at, and abused.
I've been put down, stepped on, kicked, and used!
All this anger, hurt, this naggin' pain,
This bondage over me drove me insane!

(Spoken) Oh, yes, I've felt the shame! But now I'm free,
as you can see. I'm liberated now!
I'm the victim, no longer, but a Victorious Survivor!
I came out better, stronger.
I'm a victim no more!
There's a light inside me
That'll shine and guide me
Through God's healing power
To be happy once more!

Miracle in a Potato Chip

A miracle is something that is extraordinary that cannot be explained. It is something that is spiritual in nature and surpasses human understanding.

The weekend of Palm Sunday in 2001, my husband and I were eating lunch, just sandwiches and potato chips. I reached into the bag of Lay's potato chips and could hardly believe my eyes when I pulled out a huge chip. As I looked at the chip, I saw in it what looked like one of the flowers around my mailbox, a fully formed pansy. I held the chip up to the light for my husband to see and asked him what he saw.

"A pansy," he answered.

I carefully put the potato chip in a plastic bag because there is a great significance in a pansy for me. A pansy reminds me not only of springtime, but also of God's love.

The Message in a Pansy

Along with belonging to the Christian Motorcyclists Association, my husband and I have a ministry out of our home. We call it "His Mission." It is an outreach to ex-cons, drug addicts and emotionally wounded people.

In 1996, I wrote a letter to a man in prison to whom we have ministered for several years and slipped in a dried pansy for him to put in his Bible to remind him of God's love. This is what I wrote:

Here is a pansy from our garden. The white is to remind you of purity. As you are able to ask forgiveness from God, you will be able to forgive yourself, and He will make you pure.

The pansy needs the nourishment of the earth to grow and flourish, just as each of us needs God's Word to grow to be more like Him.

And just as the pansy needs the rain, or water, to grow and be beautiful, we need Jesus to shower us with His blessings as we allow Him to reign in our lives.

The pansy needs the sun, just as we need the Son of God so that we can become the kind of child of His that He created us to be.

Differing Opinions

As friends have come to our home over the years, I have shown some of them my potato chip and asked them to tell me what they see. Some have seen things other than a pansy in the potato chip. That reminds me that God speaks to each of us individually, as well as collectively when we are His children. There are messages from God to each of us that defy explanation or rationale. All that we need can be found in His Word, but He delights in surprising us with spiritual truths in some unusual ways—many of them miracles, to be sure.

There are people who think God lives in a box in Heaven, but you can't prove that by me. He is active and involved in my life moment by moment, delighting me with Himself and His truths.

Post Script

My photographer husband took a picture of the potato chip. He laid it on the wooden windowsill so light could come in on it while he took the picture. When we got the picture back, both of us were shocked at what we saw. The mullions that divide our windows into smaller sections formed a cross in between the potato chip and the window, once again reminding us that God often presents His miracles to us in very mysterious and surprising ways.

Photo Copyright by Wayne Hansen

BECOMING AN AUTHOR

In Isaiah 61, Isaiah says that God had commissioned him "to bind up the brokenhearted, to proclaim freedom for the captives and release from darkness for the prisoners, . . . to comfort all who mourn, and provide for those who grieve in Zion—to bestow on them a crown of beauty instead of ashes, the oil of gladness instead of mourning, a garment of praise instead of a spirit of despair."

God has done in my life what He promised Isaiah. He has healed me and allowed me to reach out with that same healing ministry to others.

Turning Point

A turning point in my life came during the summer of 1999, when I was able to face the youth pastor who had molested me forty-four years before then. It was something I had never even thought about doing, but God orchestrated it for me. *When He opens a door, you definitely need not kick it open!*

One of the last things the pastor who headed the committee of discipline and restoration said to the seventy-one-year-old sex offender was, "Listen to the cries of the children."

He responded quietly, "I am."

A New Way to Minister

Coming home from that experience released my speaking and writing abilities that had been birthed out of my pain.

The pastor's phrase, "listen to the cries of the children," stuck with me. My working title for an article I wrote was "Listen to the Cry of the Child . . . the Silence is Deafening!" I knew that if I ever wrote a book about my experiences, that would be its title. It was in the spring of 2002 that I was able to commit this book manuscript to the computer.

The editor of *Alliance Life*, a worldwide magazine, changed the title of my article to "Breaking the Silence," and the two-page article was in the May 2002 issue. Our youngest son, Jonathan, illustrated the article with the sketch on the cover of this book of a little girl with a big tear inching down her cheek as she clutches her teddy bear.

When I first saw Jonathan's sketch, I started weeping. Not only does the little girl look like me, the picture also took me back to my childhood and the house of the older family member who had molested me. I was filled with remorse and shame as I remembered this wounded tiny little girl crying in her bed and wondering if anyone heard my cries.

In telling my story, I am writing others as well. I recognize this as a gift from God my Father. In giving back to others, I heal a part of myself. *Your outsides won't be normal until your insides begin to heal!*

The more I write, the more inspired I become, and the more I *have to write!* I can't really explain it, except that an artist is never really done. Whether the artist paints, writes, draws or makes music, he is never done. *It comes from something deep inside!* If this is helping me come to wholeness and freedom in Christ, it can help others begin to heal their spirits too. Then I thought about the cross and how far I had come and how I could help others.

> Though your sins are like scarlet, they shall be as white as snow; though they are red as crimson, they shall be like wool.
> —ISAIAH 1:18

Mother Teresa once said, "The only way you can give as Jesus did is to give out of your brokenness . . . out of your pain!" Jesus wants us loosed, not bound. And He calls us, as wounded people, to be His stretcher-bearers to help those who are hurting. As Jesus was dying, He was giving life to the thief on the cross. Matthew 18:18 says that "whatever you bind on earth will be bound in heaven, and whatever you loose on earth will be loosed in heaven."

Sympathy simply says, "I'm sorry." Empathy is deeper. It gets inside the other person's shoes and walks with him or her in the healing process. I believe this is one of the reasons God has called me to minister to those who are in so much pain because of unresolved trauma in their lives. I understand the pain these people are in as they make such destructive lifestyle choices. God has healed me, and I can extend that healing to others in His name.

> You who have endured the stinging experiences
> are the choicest counselors God can use.
>
> —CHARLES SWINDOLL

THE BIRD
FLIES FREE

And even the very hairs of your head are all numbered. So don't be afraid;
you are worth [far] more than many sparrows.

—MATTHEW 10:30–31

One who has been sexually abused hates dark houses, loves open
windows, hates closed doors and the cold dark days of winter, loves
spring and new growth. With the simple wonder of a child, I love
my beautiful flower gardens, getting my hands in the dirt to plant tiny seeds,
and watching green shoots come up. The more time I spend outdoors in
summer, the better I feel.

Everything comes alive in my gardens. Baby robins try out their tiny
wings for the first time, butterflies emerge from cocoons and the bumble-
bees get nectar from my lavender iris.

In anticipation of spring 2002, I painted several birdhouses in bright
greens, blues and reds. The birds nested in my forsythia bush, fed at the
birdfeeders, drank from the hummingbird nectar and took baths in the bird-
bath. We woke up every morning to the chirping sounds of various kinds of
birds.

Then when I had completed the first draft of this manuscript, my husband surprised me with a very unique birdhouse. Made out of copper and
tin, it is round and has a pointed shingled tin roof, and has an open door.

He didn't realize the significance this gift had for me. When birds' feathers are clipped like the brightly colored parrots in a pet shop, they can't fly. That is how I felt until God began to heal me.

As I complete this manuscript, I give praise to God my Father. This child is now free to fly—at last!

Set me free from my prison, that I may praise your name.
—PSALM 142:7

But he knows the way that I take; when he has tested me, I will come forth as gold.
—JOB 23:10

FORGIVENESS

Bless those who persecute you. . . . Do not be overcome by evil, but overcome evil with good.

— ROMANS 12:14, 21

Love your enemies and pray for those who persecute you.

— MATTHEW 5:44

If you are offering your gift at the altar and there remember that your brother has something against you, leave your gift there in front of the altar. First go and be reconciled to your brother; then come and offer your gift.

— MATTHEW 5:23–24

I cannot write this book without including a chapter about forgiveness. God knows the path we take and knows everything we have experienced. His command is always that we forgive.

Forgiveness was the last step I had to take on my journey to freedom.

Explaining Forgiveness

I recently dialed 911 by mistake. My husband has 911 programmed into the speed-dial feature of our phone for my safety in the intense work we do with ex-offenders.

Even though I told the 911 operator I had made a mistake by punching the wrong speed-dial button, the police department must follow up on every call.

I was cleaning our pool as the officer drove up the driveway. I apologized for my call, and he told me he was glad it was only a mistake. He admired the pool, the workmanship of our beautifully laid brick walkway, the abundant flower garden, and the new white picket fence my husband had just made for me.

He looked familiar, and after we had chatted for a few minutes, I asked him if we had ever met. He said that he had responded to a call to our home several years before when we had been the victims of a break-in forced entry robbery at our home. All of our jewelry and most of my husband's professional photography equipment had been stolen at that time. I went on to explain that we had been very frightened by that experience. It had no doubt been the work of drug dealers, the very kind of people to whom we were now reaching out. I told him we have a mission out of our home to drug dealers and ex-offenders. He looked shocked and asked if we were paid by the state.

"No," I said. "We do it for the sheer joy of doing it! As we began to reach out to them, God cleaned up our act! God works in very mysterious ways when we are obedient to His call."

I think he thought I was crazy, and I offered to give him a copy of my recently published testimony.

As I easily shared a small portion of my testimony with him, his response surprised even me: "Wow! We see many victims at the police department that have been brutally abused. You were victimized, but you also forgave him?"

All I could tell him was that only because of God's forgiveness and grace freely extended to me was I able to do that. How could I expect him to understand it when sometimes I can't understand—let alone explain—God's infinite mercy and love?

The Need to Forgive

Proverbs 14:16 says, "A wise man fears the LORD and shuns evil, but a fool is hotheaded and reckless." Anger and an unforgiving spirit on our part can become a poison in our relationships with others and God Himself.

We cannot even approach the Father if we are not at peace with others. Maybe our wounds are still too fresh and bleeding. Maybe we haven't forgiven ourselves for what we have done.

Most of us have been hurt by others. Forgiveness does not forget what was done to us because the pain is so deep and the scars remain. But as we begin to heal within ourselves, the pain will lessen. In fact some of those deep wounds can even be "gifts in disguise," as they have been in my life. I would never be this fulfilled and peaceful if I had not been able to forgive.

> **Forgiving does not erase the bitter past.**
> **A healed memory is not a deleted memory.**
> **We change the memory of our past into a hope for our future.**
> **—Lewis Smedes**

It doesn't mean that we condone what was done to us. Those who have harmed us will have to answer to God, to others, and to themselves. God forgives them, too, when they ask for His forgiveness.

The more I read in scripture about how deeply Jesus was hurt, betrayed, spit upon, spoken against and despised—*and yet He forgave*—the more I realize that forgiveness is not a weakness. It is a strength! When we hide from forgiveness, we are really hiding from ourselves. Some of us spiral deep into the darkness of the bondage of the drug world, alcoholism, food, fantasy, sexual addictions, or work and live a crippled life. Jesus wants us to live a life of freedom!

The dictionary defines *victim* as "one who is injured, destroyed or sacrificed under any of various conditions." That would include things like cancer, rage, desire, ambition, as well as mental, psychological, physical, or sexual abuse.

Truth must be restored to us. Jesus is the truth. He said, "I am the way and the truth and the life" (John 14:6). We must be willing to face ourselves and come clean, being honest about our pasts in order to free ourselves from the past. When we free ourselves, we are able to forgive.

In the twelve steps in the recovery process, the first step is "admission that our lives have become unmanageable."

New International Version Recovery Devotional Bible

My *New International Version Recovery Devotional Bible* has been like life for me. It is unlike any other Bible I have ever read. When I was younger, I memorized scripture for years just to get free weeks at youth camp. I will always have those verses from the King James Version imbedded in my mind, but when I needed life brought back to this wounded child, the *New International Version Recovery Devotional Bible* ministered to me by God's Spirit in a way I could not believe.

It is a unique tool for those of us who need healing or are recovering from addictive, compulsive or codependent behavior patterns. It weaves together the Bible text, the set of principles used in Alcoholics Anonymous (AA), Adult Children of Alcoholics (ACOA), Codependents Anonymous, and other twelve-step groups.

The scriptures brought me spiritual truth, and the "Life Connections" and "Meditations" sections brought me practical truth. The twelve steps are based on biblical principles, and many churches have incorporated them into their support and recovery programs.

The Twelve Steps

From the Alcoholics Anonymous website (brackets mine):

1. We admitted we were powerless over alcohol [or other addictive behaviors, including drugs, sex, work, food, etc.]—that our lives had become unmanageable.
2. We came to believe that a Power greater than ourselves could restore us to sanity.
3. We made a decision to turn our will and our lives over to the care of God as we understood Him.
4. We made a searching and fearless moral inventory of ourselves.
5. We admitted to God, to ourselves and to another human being the exact nature of our wrongs.
6. We were entirely ready to have God remove all these defects of character.
7. We humbly asked Him to remove our shortcomings.
8. We made a list of all persons we had harmed, and became willing to make amends to them all.
9. We made a direct amends to such people wherever possible, except when to do so would injure them or others.
10. We continued to take personal inventory, and when we were wrong, promptly admitted it.

11. We sought through prayer and meditation to improve our conscious contact with God as we understood Him, praying only for knowledge of His will for us and the power to carry that out.
12. Having had a spiritual awakening as the result of these steps, we tried to carry this message to alcoholics [and others], and to practice these principles in all our affairs.

A Process

Forgiveness is a process that begins with the first step of admitting we need God's help to light the darkness. It is an act of our will. The second step, believing that a power greater than ourselves can restore us to sanity, brings us to the altar of surrender where God does something deep inside us.

If we feel we can't go to the person who harmed us or even pray for that person, perhaps we need to pray for ourselves. God can do what we in our own mind and heart don't feel like we can do. He does it through His Holy Spirit when we open our hand and give it to Him.

The dictionary defines *anger* as a strong feeling of displeasure and belligerence aroused by a real or supposed wrong—grief, wrath, exasperation, resentment, fury, strong feelings aroused by injury, injustice, or wrong. Anger is a sudden, violent displeasure, accompanied by an impulse to retaliate.

Fury goes even deeper. It is a rage so great it resembles insanity!

Gandhi once said, "If we live an eye for an eye, the world would be blind!"

"He brought them out of darkness and the deepest gloom, and broke away their chains" (Psalm 107:14). That's what forgiveness does!

When we come to the altar, we come by faith and put the burden down. If we insist on holding on to pain and unforgiveness, they become like a noose around our necks that will eventually strangle us. Our anger, our sadness and our holding on to grief destroy our spirits. We must make a decision to open our clenched fist and let the burden go.

We do our part. God will do the rest, but it has to begin with the individual. We move from being a victim to becoming a victorious Christian. Forgiveness allows us to free our own imprisoned spirits and see ourselves as God does. Satan wants to keep us bound and tie us in knots. Jesus sets us free!

Then you will know the truth, and the truth will set you free.
—JOHN 8:32

The Need for Time in Forgiveness

"When we pressure victims to let go of the anger quickly and forgive the perpetrator [or anyone else for that matter!], we don't realize that premature forgiveness can actually hinder the healing process. Often the Christian community doesn't know how to deal with these issues. Some people in the church don't understand that anger is a natural response to being sexually abused and is a defense against being hurt again" (brackets mine).

This above quote is from Jeanette Vought, Ph.D. She is a licensed psychologist and marriage and family therapist, a certified criminal justice specialist, and the founder and executive director of The Christian Recovery Center in Minneapolis, Minnesota. She and Lynn Heitritter co-authored *Helping Victims of Sexual Abuse: A Sensitive, Biblical Guide for Counselors, Victims and Families*. I read this quote in *Learning to Trust Again: A Young Woman's Journey to Healing from Sexual Abuse* by Christa Sands and Joyce K. Ellis. I recommend both books.

ARE YOU SEARCHING?

Everyone has a God-shaped hole that only God can fill. You've heard me say that several times in this book. And you've also heard me refer to "The Four Spiritual Laws." Religion is just a set of rules. Christianity is a walk of life with a God who saves.

The Four Spiritual Laws

Law 1—God **loves** you and offers a wonderful **plan** for your life.

"God so loved the world that He gave His one and only Son, that whoever believes in Him shall not perish but have eternal life" (John 3:16).

"I came that they might have life, and might have it abundantly [a full and meaningful life]" (John 10:10).

Law 2—Man is **sinful** and **separated** from God.

"All have sinned and fall short of the glory of God" (Romans 3:23).

Man was created to have fellowship with God; but, because of his own stubborn self-will (what the Bible calls sin), he chose to go his own independent way, and fellowship with God was broken.

"The wages of sin is death [spiritual separation from God]" (Romans 6:23).

God is holy and man is sinful. A great gulf separates the two. Man is continually trying to reach God, but he inevitably fails.

Law 3—Jesus Christ is God's **only** provision for man's sin. Through Him you can know and experience God's love and plan for your life.

"God demonstrates His own love toward us, in that while we were yet sinners, Christ died for us" (Romans 5:8).

He is the only way to God. "Jesus said to him, 'I am the way, and the truth, and the life; no one comes to the Father but through Me'" (John 14:6).

Law 4—We must individually **receive** Jesus Christ as Savior and Lord; then we can know and experience God's love and plan for our lives.

"As many as received Him, to them He gave the right to become children of God, even to those who believe in His name" (John 1:12).

Receiving Christ involves turning to God from self (repentance) and trusting Christ to come into our lives to forgive our sins and to make us what He wants us to be.

We receive Jesus Christ by **faith**, as an act of the **will**.

You can receive Christ right now by faith through prayer. The following is a suggested prayer:

Lord Jesus, I need You. Thank You for dying on the cross for my sins. I open the door of my life and receive You as my Savior and Lord. Thank You for forgiving my sins and giving me eternal life. Take control of my life. Make me the kind of person You want me to be.

(Taken from "Have You Heard of the Four Spiritual Laws?" © Copyright 1965, 1994, 2000 by Bill Bright. Published by NewLife Publications, Orlando, FL. Used by permission. All rights reserved.)

Order Your Own Copy

You can view the entire text of this booklet in English at www.campuscrusade.com/fourlawseng.htm.

The 16-page booklet in its entirety is also available in Spanish as well as a bilingual English/Spanish version from:

NewLife Publications
Box 620877
Orlando FL 32862
www.nlpdirect.com
1-800-235-7255

You can also contact NewLife for other helpful materials for your Christian growth.

My Word Picture

Picture yourself at your own childhood birthday party. You have invited all of your friends to the party and each child has brought you a special present. The gifts are all piled in front of you, just waiting for you to open them. But if you do not open them, they are not truly yours. You can't enjoy them without receiving them and opening them. So, each of us must open up the gift of salvation that Jesus offers and receive Him into our hearts.

KEEPING KIDS SAFE

Signs of Child Abuse

Most experts agree these are good indicators that abuse may be occurring:

- Unusual shyness or privacy regarding the body. Not wanting to undress in front of others at proper times (in a locker room or at a friend's sleepover) may indicate feelings of an "unclean" body, or an attempt to hide telltale physical marks.

- Sudden, extreme changes in behavior such as:

  * reverting to bed-wetting or thumb-sucking
  * withdrawal
  * loss of appetite
  * nightmares
  * running away
  * failing at school
  * fear of adults, a particular person or place

- Unusual interest in or knowledge of sexual matters, or expressing affection in ways that are inappropriate for a child that age. If a child is found instructing other children in sex-related play, he or she may be reenacting their own real-life situation.

- Torn or stained underclothing.

- Bleeding, abrasions, or swelling of the genitals or mouth.

Also, take note if you notice anyone showing affection to a child that appears sexual in nature, or making remarks in terms of sexual attractiveness about the child's body.

Some Statistics to Consider

From my experience and all my reading on the subject, I have come to the following conclusion: No family has been untouched by sexual abuse. You either know of someone who has been molested or someone in your family has been affected by sexual abuse. If you don't think so, you just don't know about it.

- **The National Center on Child Abuse and Neglect** in Washington, D.C., estimates that every year in the United States more than 100,000 children are physically abused, more than 60,000 are sexually abused, and more than 1,000 die from abuse and neglect by their parents.

- "Pedophiles molest an average of 120 kids before being caught or arrested." **From "Who's Coaching Your Kid?" a special report on youth sports in** Sports Illustrated **and quoted in** Charisma, **May 2000.**

- As much as 89 percent of *all* sexually abusive events occur in a relationship with a family member or with someone else known by the victim. (About 29 percent of sexually abusive events happen with a family member) Only about 11 percent of all sexual abuse is perpetrated by a stranger. **From** The Wounded Heart: Hope for Adult Victims of Childhood Sexual Abuse **by Dr. Dan B. Allender.**

- **From** Leadership, **summer 1997:**

   * The average victim of child sexual abuse is between 8 and 11 years old.

* 1 of every 5 girls and 1 of every 8 boys is sexually abused by age 12.
* Some experts estimate that 5 or 6 children in a typical classroom of 30 have been affected by sexual abuse, regardless of geographic area, race, or socioeconomic class.
* Men are responsible for from 90 to 97% of currently reported abuse cases.
* Between 60 and 90% of victims of child sexual abuse are girls.
* Offenders are not usually strangers; 70 to 80% of offenders are known to children.
* The average length of an incestuous relationship is 3 years; it is rarely a one-time occurrence.
* In the U.S., it's estimated that from 200,000 to 500,000 children are sexually abused each year; only 100,000 of these cases are reported.

- **From Dr. Drew Pinsky**, a medical doctor: "The most serious issue [about child abuse] is that traumatic experiences in childhood can actually alter the physiology of our brains and have a profound influence on our emotional development and future interpersonal behavior."

- **From other sources:**

    * Incest is an act of violence.
    * Sexual abuse is the most common of all crimes.
    * Every 2 minutes, a child is molested.
    * Victims are 4 times more likely than the general population to be depressed and commit suicide.

How Can We Keep Children Safe?

Ignoring abuse doesn't change the situation. As a society, we have ignored our innocent children for too long. They need protection and cannot do it alone. It is of utmost importance to offer assurance, love and trust if you suspect a child is being abused. Children almost never make up these things and must be believed.

Don't act shocked at what they tell you. Let them know you're glad they told you. Teach your children that if someone says, "Don't tell!" that it is OK to tell you. A child must feel safe in telling you, as their parent or caregiver, anything.

Teach them the difference between a "good touch" (appropriate hugs, a kiss or holding the hand of a family member) and a "bad touch" (something that does not feel right or makes them feel bad).

The American Psychological Association offers the following suggestions to parents that may help protect children from sexual abuse:

- Do not force your children to give relatives hugs and kisses. Let the child decide who is worthy of their affection.
- Develop strong communication skills with your children. Encourage them to ask questions and talk about their experiences—all experiences.
- Teach your children basic sexual education. Teach them that no one should be allowed to touch the private parts of their body.
- Teach them that adults who make sexual advances against a child are breaking the law.
- If you're not comfortable talking about sex with your children, find a health professional to do so.
- Explain to a child the importance of reporting abuse to you or someone they trust.
- Always know your children's friends and their families.
- Make sure your children know never to get into a car with anyone without your permission. (My added note to this point: *Make sure that the person driving, or a passenger in the vehicle, is not someone who is molesting your children.* This is one of the places the older family member molested me and exposed himself to me)

Reporting Abuse

If you know of a child who is being molested, it is your legal and moral responsibility to report that abuse to the authorities. You can do that by calling your local police department. They have officers who do nothing except work with victims and their families and try to bring perpetrators to justice. You can also call the National Child Abuse Hotline at 1-800-422-4453.

Resources

These books are listed in no particular order. Unless noted, they were all available from Christian Book Distributors (www.christianbook.com) as of October 1, 2002.

Healing Damaged Emotions by David Seamands, Cook Communications (workbook also available)

Healing of Memories by David Seamands, Cook Communications

The Wounded Heart: Hope for Adult Victims of Childhood Sexual Abuse by Dan B. Allender, NavPress (workbook also available)

The Healing Path: How the Hurts in Your Past Can Lead You to a More Abundant Life by Dan B. Allender, Waterbrook Press

A Door of Hope by Jan Frank, Thomas Nelson. This is a realistic story of recovery and hope by a victim of incest.

Woman, Thou Art Loosed! by T.D. Jakes, Walker and Company

Learning to Trust Again: A Young Woman's Journey of Healing from Sexual Abuse by Christa Sands, Barbour and Company

Released from Shame: Moving Beyond the Pain of the Past by Sandra Wilson, InterVarsity Press

Dorie, the Girl Nobody Loved by Doris Van Stone, Moody Press

Healing from Sexual Abuse by Kathleen, InterVarsity Press

It Should Never Happen Here: A Guide for Minimizing the Risk of Child Abuse in Ministry by Ernest Zarra, Baker/Revell

Safe Place: Guidelines for Creating an Abuse-Free Environment, edited by Marv Parker, Christian Publications, the publishing arm of the Christian and Missionary Alliance. This manual is designed to assist local church leaders in developing clear policies and procedures that promote a safe and secure ministry environment in relation to abuse issues. It is not intended to be a "one-size-fits-all" document, but rather a resource of information. Order directly from Christian Publications: 1-800-233-4443, or www.christianpublications.com. You can write them at: 3825 Hartzdale Drive, Camp Hill PA 17011.

A Safe Place: Beyond Sexual Abuse by Jan Morrison, Shaw Books

Beyond the Darkness by Cynthia A. Kubetin and James D. Mallory, Jr., M.D., Rapha Publishing/Word Publishing. This book can be ordered directly from Rapha Publishing/Search Resources, 1-800-460-4673 or www.crosslifebooks.com. You can also write Search Resources at: 2323 Clear Lake Blvd., Suite 180–300, Houston TX 77062.
This wonderful book can be used as the study guide for a support program, which is how I use it in the group I facilitate. Or, it can be used by an individual for personal study, which is how I was introduced to it. This book exposes the false beliefs about abuse and pulls no punches about its overwhelming effects on the life of its victim. It reveals the difficult road to recovery through the Word of God as it traces the path from victim to survivor to thriver.

Low-cost booklets that can be purchased from the American Tract Society, P.O. Box 462008, Garland TX 75046, 1-800-548-7228, or www.atstracts.org:
"Incest, the Family Secret"
"Raped and Pregnant: Three Women Tell Their Stories"

"Touching the Untouchables (AIDS)"
"Walking in Darkness: Trusting When You Cannot See"
"Walking Out of Homosexuality"

ABOUT THE AUTHOR

God has brought **Barbara Joy Hansen** through *"the valley of the shadow of death"* during the painful circumstances and seasons of her life, into the light of His love and joy. In seeking the courage to face her fears, He carried her out of the darkness into the place of becoming a *"victorious survivor!"* A victim of sexual abuse, infertility, and marriage betrayal, Barb loves compassionately and with deep empathy those who have been brutally wounded by this world.

Brought up in a pastor's home, Barb's parents were also missionaries to Sydney, Australia with the Christian and Missionary Alliance denomination. Decades went by before she realized why she invested in the protection of children, teaching them in various ministries such as Sunday School, Junior Church, Pioneer Girls, Youth Groups, Kid's Choir, and her nannie job.

Barbara and her husband, Wayne, work within prisons, drug rehabilitation programs, homeless shelters, inner-city street ministry, and Christian Motorcyclists Association in mentoring those recovering from their addictions. In a non-profit organization they have named "His Mission" from their home, they co-partner with other ministries to connect those with life-controlling problems to drug rehab programs, providing them with a church family and helping them re-enter society. Barb also teaches a fourteen-week support group "Beauty Out of Ashes" (Isaiah 61:3) using principles from Scripture and *Beyond the Darkness,* a book by Cynthia A. Kubetin and James Mallory, M.D., to help abuse victims get to the root issues of their pain.

They attend First Congregational Church in Hopkinton, Massachusetts. Barb easily shares her testimony wherever the Lord opens doors to give awareness of sexual abuse and to be a *"voice for victims!"* Their three grown sons and their families live nearby in the Boston area.